Sincerely
SEEN

Sincerely SEEN

Healing and Hope for
Your Heart, Mind, and Soul

Kathleen Mason

KINGDOM LIFE PUBLISHING

SINCERELY SEEN: Healing and Hope for Your Heart, Mind, and Soul

Copyright © 2023 by Kathleen Mason

All rights reserved under International and Pan-American Copyright Conventions. Reproductions or translation of any part of this work beyond that permitted by section 107 or 108 of the 1976 United States Copyright Act is unlawful. Requests for permissions should be addressed to:

Kingdom Life Publishing
P.O. Box 389
Colbert, WA 99005

To contact the author, write to: publisher@kingdomlifepublishing.com

U.S.A.

All Scripture quotations, unless otherwise indicated, are taken from the Holy Bible, New Revised Standard Version Bible, copyright © 1989 National Council of the Churches of Christ in the United States of America. Used by permission. All rights reserved worldwide.

ISBN 978-1-7362697-3-2

Cover artwork by Michelle Acosta
Interior design and typeset by Katherine Lloyd
Printed in the United States of America

"Sometimes, it can be difficult to follow a crucified-before-resurrected Lord! With powerful storytelling, deep reflections on the Gospels, and evocative questions from her own faith journey, Kathy Mason shows the reader how there is no glory before the cross and yet Jesus is always with us."

—*John DelHousaye, PhD*
Professor of Biblical & Theological Studies,
Arizona Christian University

"In reading Kathy Mason, one is reading a disciple of Jesus Christ who really loves him and wants, with all of her heart and mind, to serve him. Her devotion shines through almost every single sentence she writes. Most of us who write Christian literature write with a sincere devotion to Jesus. But Kathy writes with a sincerely overflowing devotion to him. I warmly recommend this, her devotional."

—*Dr. Frederick Dale Bruner*

"This book reminds us our journey with Jesus is intended to be a slow, one-step-at-a-time, intentional journey over time. She leads us on a journey of hope because we follow the risen Jesus Christ who conquers, rescues, and transforms! Kathy uses the storytelling of the Gospels to reveal the stillness of seeing Jesus for who Jesus is. When we are tempted to believe our faith is all about the doing, Kathy reminds readers it is also about seeing Jesus clearly and being found by Him."

—*Dr. Tanita Maddox*

"Kathy Mason is a legend in our community. She had poured her life into generations of young people and adults—me included. In *Sincerely Seen*, she shares decades of stories and insights learned from the trenches of ministry, the pages of Scripture, and upon her knees in prayer. She challenges readers to ask: What will it take for you to see Jesus and to be sincerely known by Him? By the end of the book you will know more than ever that you are sincerely seen and loved by Jesus."

—Dr. Sean McGever (PhD, University of Aberdeen) is area director for Paradise Valley Arizona Young Life and an adjunct faculty at Grand Canyon University. He is the author of several books, including *The Good News of Our Limits: Find Greater Peace, Joy, and Effectiveness through God's Gift of Inadequacy.*

"Kathy offers winsome, probing, and grace-filled reflections on Scripture. Some people have an acute realism about life but offer little hope. Some have a faux hope that does not properly address the present realities of living east of Eden. Kathy delightfully mixes her persistent trust in Jesus with a realism that takes seriously the brokenness of our world."

—David George Moore
Author and Host of Moore Engaging

"With *Sincerely Seen*, Kathy Mason beautifully invites the reader to sit in the hope and truth and life found in the resurrection of Christ. Through biblical stories, decades of ministry experience, and her own personal experiences of brokenness, Kathy gently positions the reader toward the ultimate hope for all who believe that Jesus is alive."

—Kyle DiRoberts
author of *The Secret to Prayer: 31 Days to a More Intimate Relationship with God* and professor of Biblical and Theological Studies, Arizona Christian University.

Contents

Introduction..1
Setting the Scene (Seen) What Was It Like, and What Will It Take?...7
1   Immediately..13
2   Secretly Waiting.....................................18
3   One Step at a Time 22
4   Rest Again?..25
5   Stone Rolled Away....................................28
6   Looked Up and Saw....................................31
7   Dark Tombs 34
8   Inside Out 37
9   Tremors and Ecstasy 39
10   Love Beyond..42
11   Flipping of Carts 46
12   Foxhole of Rebuke....................................50
13   Word and Deed, Indeed!...............................56
14   The Wonder of First Fruits...........................60
15   Come and See...65
16   Bookends of Beholding Grace!.........................71
17   Roller Coaster Ride..................................74
18   Assembling with Elders?..............................78
19   A Mountainous Moment 82
20   Breathe Easy, All Authority Is Jesus 85
21   BEHOLD HIM!..87
22   Cookies or Dirt?.....................................91
23   The LIVING ONE 96
24   Not a Moment to Lose!...............................102
25   What If?..106

26	A Seven-Mile Walk	111
27	A Cleopas Moment	115
28	Necessary to Suffer	120
29	Remember	123
30	Sacred Meal	125
31	Cooking for the King	128
32	Seven-Mile Run!	132
33	An AHA Moment!	136
34	Merry Christmas…Even If It's Not!	140
35	The Eagle's Review	146
36	Wrapped Up in Sine Cera–ity	148
37	Broken and Hidden Matzah	151
38	Regular, Normal, Everyday Life	157
39	You Are My All in All	161
40	There You Are _____	166
41	Battle Scars to Glory	169
42	Unless Ultimatums	174
43	A Scene to Be SEEN	179
44	Transformation to Melody Halls	183
45	The Good Ole Days!	188
46	Silence to Frenzy, Nothing to Greatness	192
47	Sincerely Seen by a Charcoal Fire	197
48	The Breakfast of Loving Tightly and Holding Loosely	202
49	Uncovered and Loved	205
50	The 2-C Dilemma	210
51	The Living God	215
52	Oh, How Great!	219
53	Epilogue: As Eagles Fly!	223
54	Epilogue: All Together in One Place—Happy Birthday!	228

The Finish of Scenes *(Seens)* 235
Note from the Author 239
Bibliography 241
About the Author 243

Introduction

Sincerely Seen is the title of this book. Sincerely seeing Jesus as He was, is, and will be is an interesting thought! "Sine Cera" means "without wax." Hold those thoughts!

I was honored to meet two teenagers about sixteen years ago; they would now be in their thirties. I was at a Young Life camp, working as staff, and they came driving up with their Young Life leader. Let's name them Sarah and Harris. What struck me about them was their deep friendship and their quick absorption of everything at camp that had anything to do with adventure. That's why I love teenagers and young adults. They are oh so ready for risk and adventure.

Sarah and Harris were determined adventurers and learners, and their leaders were persistent in proclaiming God's good news of life. By the end of camp, they had childlike faith in the alive Jesus Christ. Their newfound faith rocketed them into amazing hopes for their lives, including Sarah wanting to become a leader one day, as she had found great joy in helping an abandoned baby bird. She had named the bird after the camp: Woodleaf. She had nurtured Woodleaf back to health all week long. I will never forget the look of love and understanding in her eyes as she prepared to board the bus, holding the birdhouse that she and Harris had built—made of a box from the kitchen she'd been given, with food and water—or how she cared for and loved the baby bird. She had found she could be one who could bring health to another; she had heard the call of God in her life, said yes to His love, and then found her first assignment: to care for a baby bird.

Sincerely SEEN

She rushed up to hug me as she boarded the bus to leave, proudly showing me the birdhouse and the bird, when, all of a sudden, from the other side of the bus came another high schooler who wanted to have a little fun with her. He grabbed the box and ran from her. She yelled at him to bring it back, and I went running after him and told him to stop. But it was too late. He had been shaking the box.

Now, I don't want to make the boy out to be a criminal. He had his own issues. What person in this world doesn't? But I had told him to stop, and I made him hand over the box. Sarah, with tears rolling down her face and hysteria approaching, opened the box, and the fragile bird lay there—dead. What had been joy and purpose and the promise of a future was now destroyed in a few seconds by the boy who thoughtlessly wounded Sarah. I saw Sarah's face and held her in my arms. We talked to the boy, and he apologized, but Sarah was still distraught. Harris and Sarah got on that bus. She wouldn't part with the box or the bird and Sarahs' words were, "Kathy, I am taking the bird home, and I will bury Woodleaf at my house, where so much is broken."

I stood there fighting back tears and I prayed for her leaders to have strength to love and speak truth to their campers. Why, Lord? Why did this have to happen to her? Why are there so many broken kids? Why are there so many broken people? Why such destruction? I have had leaders text me while they were at camp, pleading for answers as they heard the stories of teenagers across the world. Texts like this one: "I'm really struggling this morning on how some people's lives are so easy and other people struggle their whole lives and don't catch a break. I can't wrap my mind around how that's fair at all." I understand this leader's text. I tell my own heart, "Brokenness in families doesn't take a vacation," as I continue to serve kids almost daily. I have been a Young Life leader for over thirty-eight years and I still cannot comprehend the hurt and pain that our young friends carry.

Why would I start out with a bird-in-a-box story and the

Introduction

unending story of brokenness in peoples' lives? I think the box resembles our lives in so many ways. We are either the bird, feeling tossed up and down in the life-box, or we know someone who is like that bird in the box. So many times, God is quiet in the middle of brokenness, and we just do the next thing. This devotional comes from my own brokenness and the observation of others' brokenness. My own broken life and my curiosity have caused me to dive into the Bible honestly—to really read the resurrection stories carefully.

The resurrection story of Jesus Christ is either true or false. I could not run away from my brokenness, and I had no hope. Instead, I had questions. Questions such as, "How can a good, real, loving, or in-control God really *be alive* and keep letting bad things happen?" I still have questions. I am a skeptic. I demand from God. I cry out to Him. I am also quiet with God, and I am learning to wait upon Him and hope in His being alive. As I entertain these haunting questions, that can breed anxiety in my heart and mind, I have remembered the words: *Sine Cera* and Jesus.

I am tired of life's shaming, all the lies, and all of the "shoulds" that my culture speaks to me. Even greater, I am tired of the lies that I speak to myself and probably to others. I am weary of people pressing on me their "I'll fix you" mentalities or their "you have leprosy of faith or mind, so let's talk about the weather" platitudes. I have done the same. And then I remember: *Sine Cera* and Jesus.

I can't "forgive and forget"—primarily the forget part; I am learning the forgive part. And then I remember: *Sine Cera* and Jesus.

Oh, and by the way, I am grieved by my failures to change society toward justice, with my lack of voice or my voice being too much. And then I remember: *Sine Cera* and Jesus.

This devotional is a recorded journey and a means for you, the reader, to freshly discover all the written Gospel stories of the resurrection of Jesus Christ. He was "Sincerely Seen" by his friends and is the alive Jesus, Savior and Friend. The result of this

"Sinerely Seen" truth is a life filled with hope. This hope was for the early followers of Jesus and continues to be the eternal hope for all who will believe in the alive Jesus Christ, particularly now in our everyday culture.

As a child, I came from abuse at the hands of the one I was supposed to be able to trust. I came from a story of dark and mentally deranged nights in the hands of an alcoholic father given to fits of rage and other, unspeakable things. I risk writing this despite my fears of, "Should you or should you not talk about this?" I'm choosing not to hide but also not to keep the focus on me, because there is ONE who is healing me—He is love. I remember *Sine Cera* and Jesus.

I was a "survival child." I couldn't control my environment, but I could take charge of myself and survive, climbing as high as I could in the tree by our house to escape. I tried to be numb as a teenager—hiding was my art and my way of life—but then GOD interrupted! I was faced with a question in my college years: Was Jesus really God? If He was God, then no gravestone would hold Him down; hope was and is restored, and He was and is alive. I believe that you, the reader, are sincere in your own quest for truth! It's one thing to believe Jesus died on a cross; it's quite another thing to believe He IS ALIVE!

So, what's the connection between *Sine Cera*, this devotional, and the resurrection stories of the New Testament? Thanks for holding on to that thought.

It was known in the ancient world that people who were selling their pottery would sometimes find cracks in the clay vessels they made, and so they would fill those cracks with wax. When the vessels were held to the light, those wax-filled cracks would be seen. The buyer would want a *sine* (or "without") *cera* (or "wax") pitcher, not a wax-filled pitcher because when warm liquids were poured into a vessel with wax then the wax would melt and the vessel would leak. The buyer wanted a Sincere Vessel—a Sine Cera vessel. What's amazing is the irony of all this! I think the cracks have great promise as Jesus Christ transforms us into

Introduction

His vessels of glory. This is because the cracks tell the story of that vessel. Stories of brokenness that are healed because of the hope in the sincerely alive Jesus, the Son of God, are beautiful. I promise you that I have cracks in my writings and wax in my understandings. I know you do too. I thank God for the people in my life who continue to ask me, "Kath, are you being sincere?" I promise you, there are cracks. I also promise you that I have spent a lifetime being interrupted by the alive Jesus who challenges me, through His Word, to let the wax of my "truths" be examined, and I remember that Jesus is not finished with me yet. I remember *Sine Cera* and Jesus! I remember that Jesus is sincerely alive. Jesus is *the only one who is* Sine Cera—Sincere—without wax. If Jesus is alive, then this means He is God. This also means that the people saw Him sincerely, and He saw them sincerely. Since He is God and is alive, then He sees you and I sincerely.

Over the last ten years of my life, when all my memories of my abuse came flooding back, I decided to do a study of the resurrection of Jesus Christ. I wanted to read about this because I, like the early friends of Jesus, needed to sit at the tomb. It seemed to be a safe place to start. I didn't want to hear any platitudes of how I was to be as a Christian woman, I wanted to know the truth of who Jesus was in the tomb of my story that I never wanted to remember. I know others have stories that they struggle with in their lives. Could Jesus Christ's story of being alive have a bearing on my life or your life today? Here are the questions that I continue to ask:

What was it like for those first skeptics and followers of Jesus of Nazareth when they walked around the next corner of their daily lives and saw Jesus—Sine Cera—Sincerely Seen?

What will it take for you or me to walk around that corner, taking the next step in the busyness and brokenness of life and expecting to see Jesus sincerely—"Sine Cera"—alive and real, alive and loving, alive and in control, alive and good?

At the end of each devotional, I will write a truth about the reality of the alive Jesus. These statements have been a significant part of my healing, and so I focus on them daily. I only hope this will bring you healing and hope beyond all that you have thought possible for your heart, mind and soul.

Jesus Christ is the fullness of Sine Cera!

Setting the Scene (Seen)
What Was It Like, and What Will It Take?

What was it like for those first skeptics, doubters, and followers of Jesus of Nazareth when they walked around the next corner and saw Jesus—Sine Cera—Sincerely Seen?

What will it take for you or me to walk around that corner, taking the next step in the busyness and brokenness of life and expecting to see Jesus sincerely—"Sine Cera"—alive and real, alive and loving, alive and in control, alive and good?

I left you with these questions. In this world full of disappointments sprinkled with fleeting moments of fantasy and delight, what will it take for you or me to expect Jesus? My millennial and post-millennial friends—you know, the ones with amazing genius and creativity, with raw doubt and passions, with the ability to sleep right under the nose of the professor or sit with their legs sprawled in the aisle, acting as if the classroom revolved around them—they are the ones who courageously have the out-of-the-box ideas. I have asked this question of those who have the courage to protest injustices, knock down Berlin walls, and speak up in critical conversations. I have asked the ones who expect the moon, and long to conquer living on Mars. These are the ones who live the fullness of life every day, who listen better than those who came before them, and who want to change the world for justice's sake. I have asked them through the years, and my, HOW I HAVE GROWN! So, thank you, young friends. Sincerely, thank you. And by the way, if I placate you or give the same old answers, please write me and challenge me.

Sincerely SEEN

What will it take for you to expect to see Jesus around the next corner in your neighborhood, on your campus, in your workplace, in your local bar or restaurant? What will it take for you to see Jesus and to be sincerely known by Him?

This question could have been asked almost two thousand years ago in the sleeping city of Jerusalem, when life was just carrying on for some and stopping because of the brokenness for others. The ravaging Romans who oppressed and the pious Pharisees who condoned the oppression for their own gain had equally upside-downed the simple people of that place with the crucifixion of the Jesus, the One so many loved.

But Jesus was not a victim. Jesus would give up His last breath for mankind. This Jesus, called Jesus of Nazareth by some, was the only One able to choose when his last breath would be poured forth, after He said: "Father, forgive them, for they know not what they do;" "This day you will be with me in paradise;" "Mother, behold your son; son, behold your mother;" "My God, My God, why have you forsaken me;" "I am thirsty;" "It is finished;" "Father, into Your hands, I commit My Spirit" (*New Revised Standard Version*). If Jesus was dead and remained dead, then he was just a crazy man with a deranged mission. But if Jesus had been dead and was now ALIVE, then he was, is, and will always be GOD.

For those who sincerely followed him, sincerely hoped in him, sincerely loved him, or were just curious about him, all hope was destroyed, and there was no room for dreaming of peace on earth. There was no room in Bethlehem when that Guest arrived thirty-three years before, and there was no room in Jerusalem for hope on that early dawn Sunday morning, as the sleepy city began the preparations for its feast, the Feast of First Fruits.

All slept soundly, in the city, except for a few: There was the high priest, who began his walk through the streets to the farmlands in search of the first inkling of a sprout, of the first growth of barley grain—the promise of a harvest. Then there were the guards, more qualified than normal soldiers, alert and standing at their

What Was It Like, and What Will It Take?

post at the grave of a particular Jewish criminal named King of the Jews; Jesus of Nazareth. The town slept on, except for the women whose hearts had been cruelly crushed by the crucifixion of Jesus. Just like my little friend Sarah and her bird (as written in the introduction), these women had decided to press on in the only way they knew—to do the next thing. Through the anxiety and stress of sleepless nights, they would meet and go where their Friend lay dead to anoint His body.

> What would it take for those women to walk to that grave and expect to see Jesus, His eyes deep with compassion and understanding, just around the corner? What would it take to hope? AND—Sine Cera. The question lies clear: Was Jesus "Sine Cera—Sincerely" seen or not?

Grave times demand rising hope. I look with watchful eyes at all the young people, the eighteen-to-forty-year-old people around me, waiting for quarantine to end, waiting to rise up, waiting to demand, waiting to be heard, waiting for justice, and waiting for hope. They are just like the women of Jesus' time who went to the tomb that infamous day, waiting, waiting, waiting, and then exploding out of the door with fear and passion to do the difficult job of anointing the dead body of Jesus!

Most of us are just like those men and women who lived during the time of Jesus' crucifixion: broken, fearful, and carrying great anxiety in stress-filled times. Those women walking in Jerusalem faced broken relationships, goodness versus evil, racial injustices, oppression, wars and rumors of wars, refugees, homelessness. They faced the tattered, abused, violent, and overall confusion of their own world. They were surrounded by those living in avoidance, numbing, or powerfully controlling what they could control. How very similar to the world culture now. Nothing has changed! I don't have to convince anyone that we are indeed facing grave issues, and we are desperate for hope, hope for changed lives—hope for eternity.

So, with this in mind and heart, I desire to set off with you on a study of the Scriptures of the four resurrection stories written in

Matthew, Mark, Luke, and John: the stories of eternal hope through resurrection, re-standing erect (hope and honor restored)—the stories of all-things-made-right-life-journey. These stories—these "Scenes," or "Seens," as I like to play on the words—are moments when Jesus was "Sincerely Seen." These stories are moments when the people were seen by Jesus. They describe moments in the lives of real people, and how they handled the news, "Jesus is alive." My desire would be for each of us to slow down as we read these stories, letting God's truth bathe our minds afresh so that we can experience the risen Lord Jesus Christ, pausing for a moment to:

> "Lift up your eyes on high and see: Who created these? He who brings out their host and numbers them, calling them all by name; because he is great in strength, mighty in power, not one is missing" (Isa. 40:28, *NRSV*).

I quote from Isaiah because he was an Old Testament prophet who discovered what it was like to see the God, the Ancient of Days, the Holy One. He spoke hundreds of years before that One came to live among His image-bearers. And yet Isaiah knew that all of us must "lift our eyes" off of ourselves and our situations, our turmoil, and our disappointments, to see the One who is alive beckoning all of us to follow Him and delight in Him.

Our journey will be one of reading and asking our own questions. These stories are definitely relevant, because Mark would write about interruptions. I can't think of a year in my lifetime so marked (no play on his name intended) by interruptions as 2020.

Luke had an eye for detail, and if this story is remotely true, detail is critical. There is no better person to read than Dr. Luke in a time when our medical people are our heroes and our desire for answers is so fierce; the world of Luke was the same.

Matthew wrote with his people in mind, and he challenged all of them to stop trying to fix things, and to learn to listen to the Son of God.

John—well, John is always our feeler and deep thinker; and so many of us want to understand life through our feelings. The

What Was It Like, and What Will It Take?

Gospels were most likely written first by Mark, second by Matthew, then by Luke, and finally by John. John was the friend who lived to watch all of his dear friends be martyred, and had many years to ponder the significance of the resurrected, living Jesus. John's resting place was definitely a bit like our past quarantine quarters; he is definitely relatable.

These writers, along with all of their friends, would each have their moments of incredible disbelief, shock, and wonder as they ran into the startling reality that Jesus Christ had risen from the grave. It is good to slow down and read their embarrassing stories, their incredulous stories, and their revealing stories of their real, live hearts! The very fact that they openly wrote about their doubts and embarrassing moments is evidence of the reality of the resurrection of Christ!

You have chosen to read this as you read through the Gospel stories of the resurrection of Christ. Please know that there are no "musts" or "shoulds" in this devotional. It is crucial in life to just take a resting place, read the resurrection stories, and be still. If you decide to read these devotions in a systematic manner, there are fifty-two "Scenes" and so you might want to read one a week. Or, if you want to read them all in fifty-two days, be my guest. You will notice there is an epilogue that has two "Scenes" as well. As I have written this, I have allowed myself freedom of imagination, and I have also allowed the Holy Spirit the freedom to challenge my thinking. My sources for reading and studying will be in the back of the book. Sometimes we will read and ask questions; sometimes we will imagine and wonder. Sometimes we will shout out to God, "I don't buy it!" Sometimes we will read and be comforted to know this is real.

This is what scripture does, as does the Holy Spirit. Scripture cuts through, divides, and breathes life, hope, questioning, and faith. As you read, put yourself among these first-century followers of Jesus and imagine. You might be surprised; I sure am! Ultimately, my desire is to devote this time to being rejuvenated by the Trinity and Jesus' resurrection, so that all of us might learn to live as the first-century followers of the One who called all (and calls all) by name—through the trials and the joys of life—to "come and see," as the angel at the tomb of Christ said. He really is *Sine Cera—the Sincere*! He sees us as we are; He sees and knows us sincerely. And He is calling us to see Him in these stories of resurrection, to surrender to Him and become His own sine-cera vessels, declaring to others, "He is Sine Cera—sincerely alive."

You will notice that at the end of each devotional is a statement of who Jesus is from the section. Please read these stories while thinking about who He is to you. This is the purpose of this time of reflecting on the resurrection stories of JESUS CHRIST. For it is He who would tell His friends that each bird of the field is seen by God, and if the birds of the field are seen by the Lord, how much more are we?

By the way, for those of you who read the introduction: if you are the girl who learned to believe in the Sincerely Seen, risen Lord Jesus because of God's Spirit, your leader's love for you, and a little bird that you named Woodleaf, I pray that you find great hope in knowing all things will be restored; your heart, soul, mind, and yes, even the birds, because **Jesus is alive!**

> **Prayer:** "Lord Jesus, open our eyes that we might sincerely know we are seen by You and sincerely see You as You are—ALIVE." Amen.

Scene (Seen) 1

Immediately

Mark 15:42–46

When evening had come, and since it was the day of Preparation, that is, the day before the sabbath, Joseph of Arimathea, a respected member of the council, who was also himself waiting expectantly for the kingdom of God, went boldly to Pilate and asked for the body of Jesus. Then Pilate wondered if he were already dead; and summoning the centurion, he asked him whether he had been dead for some time. When he learned from the centurion that he was dead, he granted the body to Joseph. Then Joseph bought a linen cloth, and taking down the body, wrapped it in the linen cloth, and laid it in a tomb that had been hewn out of the rock. He then rolled a stone against the door of the tomb. (*NRSV*)

Reread these verses, and then say what happened out loud.

Questions that will be raised through the devotion:
- From the perspective of Joseph, what happened?
- What choices did Joseph have, and what choices did he make?
- What were the results of the choices Joseph made?

"Immediately" never happens in creation until that moment. One waits and waits to capture the sunset, and "immediately," it disappears! "Immediately" is such a simple word and yet it was used by the author of the Gospel of Mark with great precision. "Immediately" is a crucial word in the writings of Mark, or John Mark, as he was truly named. "And it happened" is another translation, as if he were on the scene, reporting live. He may not have been a disciple, but I think he had been on the scene, trailing Peter as a little brother trails an older one, although they were not brothers. Mark was just like that: young, impulsive, explosive, and intuitive. He would write in his Gospel, "and then," or "this happened," or "immediately," almost as if he were running up to someone, out of breath, excited about a discovery he had learned.

Mark was a bullet point writer. He moved right into the adventures of Jesus and he would report the crucifixion of Jesus after fourteen short chapters. Suffice it to say that Jesus of Nazareth had been killed by being nailed to a cross; a common death penalty among Roman culture. Jesus knew it was coming, He prayed it would not happen, and He obeyed His Father through His death on a cross. Why, you might ask? Why would the One who could heal the sick, bring sight to the blind, raise the dead, and bring hope to the outcast and marginalized allow Himself to be caught, tried, whipped, and nailed to a cross, experiencing excruciation (a word that comes from "cross")? Let's wait on that deep question, and maybe, at the end, we might know the answer, for even the dead body of Jesus was compelling to those left with the question: Who was this Jesus?

The Jewish Sabbath was Saturday so the day before the Sabbath would have been Friday. All Jewish people knew that one had to hurry to finish work before Sabbath began at sundown. They also knew that any respectful Jewish friend would take care of another friend's body, and not leave it for the animals and birds of prey, as Jesus was hanging dead on the cross. Not only this but their culture would make this urgent.

Joseph of Arimathea, a religious leader, was torn in spirit and heart at this dilemma of a lifetime; if he left Jesus' body on that cross to be defiled, no respectful friend of Jesus was he, and if he went to Pilate, the Roman head, to claim the body of Jesus, he would be considered no respectful Jewish leader. Jesus had blasphemed, according to the high priest, calling Himself God: "Are You the Christ, the Son of the Blessed One?" And Jesus said, "I

Immediately

am; and you shall see the Son of Man sitting at the right hand of Power, and coming with the clouds of heaven." Tearing his clothes, the high priest said, "What further need do we have of witnesses? You have heard the blasphemy; how does it seem to you?" (Mark 14:61–64). Jesus would be led away to be crucified and the high priest would be satisfied. Jesus was considered to be a criminal who lied and called Himself God. Who cared if His body was left to be corrupted on a cross? Jesus was considered nothing but a blasphemer! Yet the thought of it pressed into Joseph's conscience, searing and scorching, until he could no longer stay secretive or silent. Joseph of Arimathea went forth to be a friend of Jesus and bury his body.

Joseph—whose possible namesake was the son of Israel and overseer in Egypt—was a Pharisee during the time of Jesus. Thousands of years before, the Joseph of the Old Testament had saved his tribal family from a famine of food, a famine of forgiveness, and a famine of family unity by risking it all: his reputation, his power, and his pride, receiving his betraying brothers and providing for them. Yes, he saved his family, Israel, until there was another Joseph about 1,470 years later, who led his wife, Mary, and son, Jesus, into Egypt to escape the certain destruction of all Hebrew sons under the age of two.

The Josephs of the Scriptures were always taking the lead in the nation of Israel, always choosing the more difficult road of life, seemingly called by a God who continued to pursue both nation and people. And now, although too silent and too late to speak up in defense of this Jesus, who was nailed to a cross, Joseph of Arimathea would gather the courage to ask for the Savior of the world's dead body so he could bury it before the sun went down.

Three things we know for sure about this Joseph: He was a prominent member of the council of religious leaders called Pharisees. He was waiting for the kingdom of God. And, according to young Mark, he had to take up courage—*talmao*, or "to bear one's self boldly" (Strongs, G5111)—extreme conduct that means no matter how much one wants to run the other way, hide, ignore, and avoid, that person stands firm to seize the moment, not be seized by it. By his actions, Joseph became one of those who said no to the world, no to himself, and yes to Jesus—even to the dead Jesus. One would only wish to have seen the surprised look on Joseph's face at the first glimpse of the resurrected Christ. One would wish to know the thoughts of "I'm so glad I did that" floating through the mind of Joseph when he stood before the risen Lord. One might even think Joseph wished he had done more. Wouldn't we all be thinking that?

No matter what, we will face these thoughts: "If only I had spoken to them, if only I had known, if only I had not said what I said or done what I did." We all face those ghosts of "if onlys." That was part of the reason Jesus died on a cross; He took our "if only" failures upon Himself. Charles Spurgeon, a nineteenth-century British minister, wrote in regards to Psalm 32, "It cost our Savior a sweat of blood to bear our load, yea, it cost him his life to bear it quite away…See what honest confession and full forgiveness will do! The gospel of substitution makes Him to be our refuge who otherwise would have been our judge" (Spurgeon, Treasury of David).

Joseph would let go of his "if onlys" when he went that evening to bury Jesus. He no longer hid; he came forward and buried Jesus. He who had been at the top of the political sphere in Judaism, the Sanhedrin, would now cast all of it aside because of Christ dying on a cross while uttering Psalm 22. Joseph would remember the Torah and decide that evening: no more hiding, no more walking with the "big guns;" he was "demoting" himself to be a follower of Jesus, and he would affiliate himself with the friends of the One crucified.

What mattered most is that he gathered his courage and stepped into the limelight, no longer under the radar of Roman rule or the Hebrew Council, and asked for the body of the dead Jesus. What he did not know was that two days later, he would see the Alive Jesus, and all of his "if onlys" would pale in the face of THE Alive Jesus, the One who took Joseph's burdens gladly.

Immediately

What are your "if onlys"? What are you looking at now that might be a moment to gather all your courage and proceed? What do you lack in your "gathering courage?" What stops you in your tracks?

Jesus would have risen whether Joseph had found the courage to ask for the body or not. The burial in the tomb made it that much more evident that, indeed, no grave, no cross, nothing on earth could contain the body of Christ, for He is God's Son resurrected to life. So lay down your "if onlys" and your "I should have done more," and gather up your courage, because indeed, He will surprise you.

What might you be invited to do by the God who sees you?

Take time now to talk out loud to the Alive Jesus. It might feel strange if this is the first time you have done this. But "gather courage" and start with that.

Jesus Christ—God of Refuge

Scene (Seen) 2
Secretly Waiting

Mark 15:47

Mary Magdalene and Mary the mother of Joses saw where the body was laid. (NSRV)

We know the story of Mary Magdalene. Tradition, and maybe rumor, had it that she was considered a prostitute, but the fact is that seven demons were cast out of her by Jesus, and she would use all of her resources to follow Jesus, listening to His teachings, observing His healings, witnessing His claims of being Son of God, Son of Man, Son of David. She believed and followed Him to the cross and beyond the grave. That was who she was: a faithful friend and follower.

Mary, the mother of Joses, was actually a mother of sons—possibly Matthew, Joses, and James, the apostle of Jesus. She, too, had an obscure name for James, her son, who was considered and called James the Less, and she was called "the other Mary" (Matthew 27:61). She was probably married to Cleopas. Cleopas, Clopas, or Alphaeus—they were all the same person (Matt. 10:3; Luke 24:18)—was the father of Matthew, James the Less, and Joses, according to the *King James Bible Dictionary*.

Whatever Mary's title was in a male-dominated world, Mark records her here, with Mary Magdalene, secretly watching to see what Joseph of Arimathea would do with Jesus' body. They had no idea of Joseph's secret meeting with Pilate, and they had no understanding of Joseph's heart to serve this dead Jesus. All they knew was that Jesus was dead; they couldn't stay away from Him, and

Secretly Waiting

they had no desire to hide in their homes like the disciples. They couldn't stay away!

Mary and Mary Magdalene had enough resources to serve Jesus' friends, and so they did (Luke 8:2–3). Mary Magdalene and the other Mary had enough love, so they had to go stand where He lay, and they had to serve with action. Mary was always okay with being called "the other Mary." She had no reason to be individually noted. She was content to show up and look at Jesus, from a distance and close-up. Jesus had no tomb of His own, no place of His own, even in death. Joseph would choose to give Jesus his family tomb. Jesus had only people of His own: Mary Magdalene, the other Mary, and a few other women, and now they were seeing Joseph stepping in to serve Jesus. Mary and Mary Magdalene would return after the Sabbath to anoint His body—their dead friend, their dead King.

The most striking moment in these verses is the SILENCE between the women peeking to see where the rich and powerful Joseph laid Jesus' body and the end of the Sabbath. The SILENCE of their souls as they knew they had to wait to anoint His body, the SILENT longings for things to be different. What would their different story look like? They couldn't imagine that it might look like the anointing of an alive Jesus, with them serving Him and His disciples, or the moments when He might call them by name and tell them not to be afraid. They remembered that Jesus valued them, laughed with them, and cried with them, and they always listened to His stories. These women were important in Jesus' kingdom of heaven on earth; they were as vitally important as His disciples because they were created by the loving God, and they were always seeking Him.

How do I know this? Well, when all else failed, when Jesus was crucified and dead, they still had their eyes on Him! In the SILENCES where waiting and hopelessness seemed to hover like a never-ending cloud of despair, and death's reality hung over their hearts and minds, they still kept their eyes on Jesus; **they were looking on to see where He was placed.**

I wait right now, in the season of COVID-19, like all of you. Waiting under the never-ending cloud of the media reporting hopelessness. So how will I wait? How do any of us ever wait? We wait much of the time. We wait for ice to melt, for trees to bloom, for Christmas and summer vacations—in our dreams! Those women waited. All their dreams were crushed, but they still waited to go serve and be with Jesus. Little did they know what lay ahead. **Could you imagine?**

And while you are thinking this through: Why is it that Mark would write about these women waiting? For after all, they were least in the Roman, Greek, and Jewish world. Why would he report about the least of these, waiting, unless he was writing real news? There is detail in truth, and Mark doesn't hold back on detail. Waiting is difficult, and waiting without hope is close to impossible. The mind obsesses; anxiety can cause shortness of breath, and usually, there is not much sleep to be had for those who wait. The simplicity of setting one's mind on an action can help; these women made plans for the end of Sabbath as they hurried back to their homes and necessary life chores.

How do you wait?

What or whom are you looking to in your daily waiting life? What presses you to still look for hope? What are you waiting for that you have little or no control over, and how do you have a heart to look outside the given clichés of life?

Maybe you are like so many who waited awhile and then said, "I quit, God isn't real." No blame here, just questions. No judgment; it's where you might be. I know many who are there.

What if the women were waiting only to be disappointed? What would be their loss? What if the women were waiting to be surprised? What would be their gain?

I am just asking, and believe me, I have weighed the losses and the gains.

LOSSES	GAINS

Selah is a great word right here. *Selah* means "rest" or "pause" in the old Hebrew language. It was used in the middle of their singing to teach them to breathe. So, *selah*. Rest in your waiting. Breathe in and breathe out, do the next thing, and then rest and wait. I have learned a practice of welcoming waiting; it is hard but good for the heart, especially at night. So welcome your feelings, acknowledge them, and then quietly whisper, "Welcome Father, welcome Son, welcome Spirit. Help me to wait."

Jesus Christ—Our Selah!

Scene (Seen) 3

One Step at a Time

Mark 16:1

When the sabbath was over, Mary Magdalene, and Mary the mother of James, and Salome bought spices, so that they might go and anoint him. (NRSV)

*R*eading this scripture, it's almost as if Mark was making it clear that they were tired of waiting for the end of the Sabbath, and so the dawn of the first day was a welcome relief to their hearts. Finally, the Sabbath was over, and the women could at least do something—anything—to feel useful as the horrendous events unfolded, and their lack of control or power was made visible with the killing of their Messiah, their King and their Champion. Finally, they could do something; they just couldn't sit around another second!

Have you ever experienced that out-of-control moment when you must just sit on your hands, still your feet, bite your lip, silence your words, and wait it out in utter helplessness?

Talk to the Lord right now about that, or write about it.

Salome is mentioned in this story by Mark. She was considered to be the mother of the sons of Zebedee—James and John—and the sister of Mary, who was the mother of Jesus. Most would agree that Salome was a "great and powerful Oz" of a mother, so bold that she would ask Jesus, in Matthew 20:20-21:

> Then the mother of the sons of Zebedee came to Jesus with her sons, bowing down and making a request of Him. And He said

to her, "What do you wish?" She said to Him, "Command that in Your kingdom these two sons of mine may sit one on Your right and one on Your left." (*New American Standard Bible*)

Salome would be walking to the tomb on that bright Sunday morning! I wonder if, as she witnessed Jesus' crucifixion, she considered what she had asked him weeks before? She was a strong and outspoken woman with every great intention of pushing her sons into power and rule. I wonder if she contemplated, as she walked that morning to Jesus' tomb, the question that Jesus had asked her, "You do not know what you are asking. Are you able to drink the cup that I am about to drink?" (Matt. 20:22). As a mother, her heart must have shuddered at what she had asked of Jesus for her sons. And yet she chose that early dawn morning to be identified by the soldiers at the tomb as "one of His friends," like Joseph—a risky move, to follow Jesus even to His tomb! On the day when she asked Jesus the ruling question, her sons had quickly responded, with zeal, "We are able!" Little did they know that very soon after that conversation, Jesus would be led down the road to Calvary. But Jesus knew: "My cup you shall drink; but to sit on my right and on my left, this is not Mine to give, but it is for those for whom it has been prepared by My Father" (Matt. 20:22).

As Salome walked through the streets of Jerusalem to the tomb, I wonder if she remembered those words. Her sons were at someone's home, hiding with the rest of the disciples. I imagine her cringing, as any loving mother would, as she remembered His words, "My cup you shall drink." What would that mean for James and John? What would this mean for all of them? How would the "cup" be "prepared" by Jesus' Father—and who was His Father?

Mark records three women walking step after step to the tomb that morning. Was Salome talking boldly, as she did in the past, or was she fearfully wondering what it all meant? No matter, first things first—she and Mary Magdalene, the other Mary, the mother of James the Less and Joses, would roll up their sleeves, walk in brave haste, and show up at the tomb to anoint their beloved Master's body, saying all the while, "Who will roll away the stone for us from the entrance of the tomb?" They would figure out that part once they got there. Maybe they could talk the soldiers into moving the stone, so that they could be about the grisly business of respecting the tradition of anointing of the dead body, even the corpse of a criminal. Whether out of sheer madness from the terror of Jesus' crucifixion, or because they had no control, or out of brave respect for His body, they took the next step and went to the tomb. Nothing could stop them. No stone, no soldiers, no grave, no terrible "cup to drink" would stop them on their mission to anoint their Master's body and unite their lives publicly with His death—these brave women, taking one step at a time.

> What have you asked of the Lord in the past that you look back on and feel grateful He said "no" or "wait?"
>
> What "cup" do you need to trust the Father, in both taking (what you go after) and receiving (what He brings to you), in your own life? What will that process look like?
>
> Maybe you don't want to trust. Maybe you are tired and weary. How do you go on today, and do what you need to do next?
>
> Have you ever thought that the very fact that you still go on, even when you are tired or weary, is actually a step of trust, an action of anointing Him?
>
> What steps do you need to take in your life right now? What is one step that you can take?

Jesus Christ—Creator of our steps— one step at a time!

Scene (Seen) 4

Rest Again?

Mark 16:2

And very early on the first day of the week, when the sun had risen, they went to the tomb. (*NRSV*)

*F*inally, they could work; rest was over! I know we have read about this, but I want to pause and rest and feel the anxiousness of wanting to just move ahead, like the women. In each of the four narratives of this glorious day, the Sabbath is mentioned. Rest was important then, and it's important today; it will always be important. God Himself rested. The Three in One rested after creating the day—the night, the heavens—the earth, the animals—the insects—the birds—the fish, the man—the woman. God rested.

I have struggled with resting, and I struggle with resting; I am a busyness addict. What about you? Some think I'm crazy; they are all about resting. But what about rest without activity or distraction? The God of the universe and beyond—what did His rest look like?

The Psalmist speaks of rest throughout the songs—the rest of music, the rest of the beat, the rest of melody, silence. We were reminded in *Scene* 2 of the description of "*selah*"—rest. **Have you ever struggled with silence?** I think we all do, going here and there, listening to this and that, checking our cell phones and social media. Silence, in our world of distraction-pollution, is so difficult.

Was it difficult for these women? They had been oppressed for their entire lives. They thought there was a rescue from waiting and suffering under Roman rule, which was life-draining, soul-stifling, and oppressive. Just when it was within their grasp, as their friend and mentor walked through the gates of Jerusalem, and the crowds yelled, "Hosanna in the Highest," their hopes were dashed so quickly. Their visions of empowerment and freedom were dashed with their friend, their savior, now dead and lying in a tomb, having experienced the ultimate embarrassment and destruction: crucifixion!

Was it difficult for these women to rest? Another name for rest might be wait. I hate waiting! How about you? I hate waiting especially in difficult situations. I imagine they had no hope as the terror and emotional trauma smacked them in the face and smashed their dreams of rescue. But then, remember, it is always comforting to be with friends when you experience trauma. It is always good to do something, anything, just to get your mind off your lack of control and the earthquakes of disappointment shattering in front of you.

I imagine the first reactions of silence wearing off was the women just wanting to gather and serve, in some capacity, the Friend they had served for at least a year. Sabbath rest probably seemed impossible at 1:00 a.m., and waiting to gather at dawn, when the Sabbath would break, seemed like forever and ever, an eternity. I imagine the ticking of the hollow minutes, the racing of their scattered minds as they faced the aloneness of silence and the Sabbath.

Now it's 2:00 a.m. If you have ever spent a night alone, you know what I am writing about. The silence is deafening. 3:00 a.m. strikes, and your heart pounds with anxiety as you long for the light of dawn, the breaking of rest.

Then 3:30 a.m. approaches, and Mary Magdalene and the women—each in her own home (and remember, there are no cell phones to text one another in the darkness)—can't sleep. Restlessly pacing in the middle of Sabbath rest, they can't even scroll their Jerusalem-grams. (OK…now that's ridiculous…I know…just had to throw it in there.) There's just aloneness, Sabbath introspection, crying out to God, and then a traumatized rest, full of visions of the crucifixion of their Friend and would-be King. I wouldn't doubt that this Sabbath, for these women in 33 AD, seemed like a neverending day; a standstill-of-time-Sabbath.

How would the Father of their hearts, the Father God of His only Son, bring Christ to life once they took Him off the cross? Why would God allow you and me to have the "dark night of the soul" the ancient writers, like John of the Cross, write about? The silence I am thinking about comes in the middle of rest, while everyone else seems busy, happy, and filled with purpose and life.

> **Sabbath—Rest—creates space. Space to ask the infinitely eternal questions: Why am I here? Why has this happened? Where are You, God? Who are You, God? Who am I?**

So, my friend, rest. Rest fitfully, rest peacefully. Just rest and wait for time to show you the Divine.

I dare you to rest for a few hours, away from all distraction. And then, when you are finished resting, rest longer. For there, in the middle of that great panic of silence and your acknowledgement that God is God and you are not, then you will know Him and know yourself more.

It even happened to those women: "When the Sabbath was over...brought spices, so that they might come." My question is "and do what?" Cry? Gather the people? Cause a revolt? No. "They might come and anoint Him."

For He is God.

Jesus Christ is Lord of the Sabbath!

I pray for silence, hard moments of silence and peaceful moments of silence, for you, my fellow sojourner. *Selah.*

Scene (Seen) 5
Stone Rolled Away

Mark 16:3

They had been saying to one another, "Who will roll away the stone for us from the entrance to the tomb?" (*NRSV*)

Reread these verses, and then say what happened out loud.

Questions that will be raised through the devotion:

What are the stones in your life—the obstacles, the blockades that frustrate you? Speak them out loud, cry them if you must, but stop hiding them or letting them embitter you.

What is it you need to hand over to the living, breath-taking, and breath-giving Father in heaven?

The women had no questions about the Roman guards, not "What if they connect us with Jesus and take us away to be crucified?" or "What do you think the guards will do; will they kill us?" Just this question: "Who will roll away the stone for us from the entrance of the tomb?"

For these women there were no meetings in a hidden room; they were abandoning all to do what they, as women, did: anoint dead bodies. This wasn't just another villager's dead body. This was their friend, their rabbi, their advocate, their Master. No questions would be asked by the guards—it was common practice, even at a rich man's tomb. Joseph of Arimathea—a councilman of the religious, a Pharisee—had come to Pilate to ask for the body. I know we have discussed this before, but I just want to point out that Joseph, a quiet man, was never once recorded as saying anything in the Scriptures, yet he is recorded in all four Gospels as the one who took Jesus' body off the cross and laid Him in the tomb on his own, assuring that Jesus' body would not be assigned to a common grave. How insignificant a task, and yet how important in the large scheme of the resurrection. There would be no confusion about this resurrection; only Jesus was buried in this rich man's tomb, and only Jesus walked out! *Insignificance is often a prelude to God's redemption!*

The women, insignificant in comparison with Jesus' disciples, did the insignificant task of waking as the sun rose on another first day of the week. The women were insignificant just because they were women in the Hebrew, Roman, and Greek world. Their chore was insignificant—anointing the dead body of a seemingly insignificant man who was triumphantly murdered by the world. The only significant thing in their lives at that moment was the stone separating their insignificant oils from their Master's dead body. Who would roll away this significant division between humanity and Jesus' holiness? That was what their minds and words were about; who would roll away the division, the statement of death, so that they could insignificantly serve their dead Master? Who would roll away that which separated them from Jesus? Whispering quietly, they rounded the corner and found the answer.

God rolled away the separation, the stone before the tomb, the declaration of death, the powerless proclamation of darkness, death, and evil. God would roll it away. Oh—the weight of the significant God who would roll away the stone, the barrier between heaven and humanity! How did God do this? How does He create the winds that shake the eighty-foot pine trees? How does God keep the oceans within boundaries? How does God heal the sick—yes, even the COVID-sick—and how does God bring sight to the blind, or cause the blind to sing to all of Italy and the world, "Amazing Grace, how sweet the sound that saved a wretch like me; I once was lost, but now I'm found, was blind, but now I see?" And by the way, thank you for singing those words on Easter, on the steps in Italy in 2020, Mr. Andrea Bocelli.

Oh, let us proclaim joy in the midst of a garden of sorrow with these women. God would roll the stone away. What a divine dream, a heavenly vision, a resurrected reality. God rolled away the stone of separation forever. Amen and Amen.

Today reflect on the questions asked in the beginning of this *Scene* 5.

> **Ask the God who moved away the stone of the tomb of Jesus to roll away the thoughts, plans, and disappointments that stand in the way of your heart rejoicing in what He has done for you; roll away the stone!**

Jesus Christ— the Completion of Amazing Grace!

And if you can't do this, then just stand in shock that the stone rolled away for these women, because it's true. And yes, you may say the disciples or someone else did it; nevertheless, the stone was rolled away, and the body was not there. You and I can think about that.

Scene (Seen) 6
Looked Up and Saw

Mark 16:4

When they looked up, they saw that the stone, which was very large, had already been rolled back. (NRSV)

The previous devotion asked the question, "What are the stones in your life?" Now I want to propose that the stones in our lives are not fictitious illustrations, but real and extremely large. A stone might be another bout with a debilitating sickness and the doctor shaking his or her head; or a woman's father telling her to get out of the house five hours after her mother dies; or a Latino father warning his teens, who are driving, to be especially welcoming if they get pulled over by the police, because their brown skin may be held against them; or two feuding parties in a church who communicate their sides of a quarrel only to walk away thinking the "other side" is lying. Or what of the woman who is told she can't be a pastor because she is a woman, or the little boy who keeps his hand in his pocket because he was born with no fingers, and there's no way the coach would ever believe he could be a good football player, or the one who stutters, or the one who is homeless, or the one who is rejected by her boyfriend's parents because she is from another country? All of these examples and more are major "stones" in people's lives, with major consequences and major hardships to be overcome.

These and the myriad other stones in our lives pressure each of us to say, "There can't be a God, because of this stone." And all the well-meaning fix-it people seem to do is crowd around us, pat us on the back, and say, "No worries, God means it all for good." I'm sorry, but though these people might have all the good intentions in the world or be great proclaimers of truth—at that moment, please, oh please, don't paste the "God means it all for good" Band-Aid on the gaping wound of brokenness and the harsh reality that, indeed, this is an extremely large stone! If God is good but not in control, then He is weak. If God is in control but not completely good, then He is not loving. It must be both. It must mean that God knew full well that there would be Large Stones and gigantic trials—but He is in control. If the trials are present, then He must have a plan if He is in control. And if these Large Stones exist, and God is good, then there must be BETTER, LARGER good that will come after it.

And for the people patting others on the head with very kind intentions—let them, let us, be still and weep with those who weep, and rejoice with those who rejoice. If God is big enough to create the LARGE STONES, He is big enough to speak to the one wondering "who will roll away the stone" of life. It is not your job, my job, or anyone's job to minimize the stone, the trauma, the suffering, the wound, or the death of whatever is dear to another's heart in the broken world.

So—without any other words, I want to just pause like young John Mark and remember that this Gospel pen is reporting the most riveting and outrageous words. He uses "sight" words twice in one sentence: "Looking up" and "they saw." The women looked up; they saw their stone rolled away, and indeed, it was an "extremely large stone." They looked up…they saw…indeed. They were *not* expecting this. They were in their own perceptions, their own truths, their own worlds, and they looked up and saw. This is monumental. In a world of harsh reality, it is crucial for us to remember to look up and see—to look up and see the sunsets, look up and see the trees. Why would Mark write these words? Perhaps because neither he nor they were expecting what was next: the extremely large stone rolled away! Oh God, give us their eyes, give us their "looked up and saw."

So—broken one, or think-you-figured-it-all-out one, or the in-between one, grieve over your losses, your extremely large, impossible-to-move stones, and cry out to God; these women did. Then wash your face and go to the stone of your heartache. Look up and talk to Jesus—yes, out loud. Then watch as the women "saw." It might take some time, but watch for the stone to be removed.

I pray for you—with words to talk and ears to listen—about the very Large Stones for all of us.

Jesus Christ—the Architect of Stones

Scene (Seen) 7

Dark Tombs

Mark 16:5

As they entered the tomb, they saw a young man, dressed in a white robe, sitting on the right side; and they were alarmed (*NRSV*).

The women were surprised, astounded, terrified, alarmed, and amazed at the sight of the tombstone rolled away, the "young men," and the empty tomb. You will notice that two of the Gospels will call them angels, and two of the Gospels will call them men." What do we do with this difference of reporting? This might pose doubt.

The theologian Dr. Dale Bruner states:

These discrepancies (as they may be called) honor the Gospel writers' fidelity to their sources and to their own convictions and freedom of expression. The early church's refusal to suppress these differences when they put together the canon of Scripture indicates a doctrine of biblical inspiration we can imitate—an inspiration that protects the message, not in details; a harmony of affirmations, not of particulars; the composition of a fugue, not a chant." (Bruner, 781-782)

Yes, details bring out the personalities of each Gospel, the very human aspect of these written stories. With no apologies, just a celebration, they are human, and they wrote according to how they saw or heard it. The beauty of difference is there is no "fixing it up;" there is no trying to make excuses. There is just raw honesty—actually a breath of fresh air in a world filled with the stagnancy of stale, monotonous religiosity and the screaming voices of doubt and the media saying, "There is no God."

> **How many times have you been amazed, astounded, or even terrified by the thought that this (whatever your "this" is) could not have happened "by chance?" How many times have you been astonished when everything just "falls into place?"**

My story: I couldn't sleep because of the memories that haunted my rest. I had spent a year working through memories of a father who abused me. I still had trouble sleeping at night. I was working one weekend at a Young Life camp and decided to go for a walk, late at night, and pray for the kids tucked away in their dorm rooms with their beloved leaders. At least then I could use the menace of late-night-awake-time for a purpose higher then fretful tossing and turning.

It was in the dead of winter, and the temperature was frigid—a picture of how I felt, with the hollow echoes in my heart of the empty, longing for a dad that I had wanted instead of the dad that I actually had. I was reflecting on that little girl of my memories, and then pressed into prayer for the kids in the dorms. Around 1:00 a.m., as I walked round and round the camp, I begged God to heal them, hoping He would heal me. Hours later, I finally went to bed. Waking the next morning and thinking through my night, I began to accept the death of what I thought had been my childhood and see what true reality was for that little girl. I asked the Lord for strength as I finished working with the Young Life staff, serving a camp of over five hundred high school kids and leaders that weekend.

No one knew of my battle the night before except for me and the God who "holds all my tears in a bottle" (Psalm 56:8). So—when I was surprised, like those women at the tomb, what did it have to do with Mark's writing of old? Later that day, I would receive a phone call from my mother, saying, "Your father woke up at one o'clock this morning, went to the bathroom, fell, and shattered his foot, and he is in the hospital. Can you come to be with me?"

This was the beginning of great healing in my heart and in the life of my mother. The trauma had placed him in the hospital, and I would go to stay with her the next week. We would spend hours together, and she would come to faith in Christ—a story left to be told. This was a large stone over a very dark tomb in my life, and I think God is very willing to bring us to these dark-tomb places for the purpose of resurrection and healing. Sometimes we see the impact of praying, and sometimes we don't, but God is not dead and lying in a tomb.

I write this story to say this: There are no coincidences, there are only God-pictured moments that occur in our lives, which bring us face to face with the possibility of a living God who is recklessly invasive and will get to the bottom of the tombs in our life for His good purpose and heart, and for our good purposes and heart. He will not stop; He wants my healing and your healing.

> So I ask you, my friend, to list the times in your life that the intimate God creatively and decisively brought you face-to-face with the dark tombs in your life, and then try to see the measure of goodness—not in your circumstances, but God's goodness, because He is good!
>
> Take the time to reflect on the stone rolled away, the young man sitting at the right and wearing a white robe, and the empty tomb. List those hard tomb places that God is beginning to open up into places of breath; breathe in and breathe out.

Jesus Christ—Conqueror of Dark Tombs!

THERE IS HOPE! HE IS NOT IN THE DEAD TOMB;
HE IS RISEN!

Scene (Seen) 8

Inside Out

Mark 16:6

But he said to them, "Do not be alarmed; you are looking for Jesus of Nazareth, who was crucified. He has been raised; he is not here. Look, there is the place they laid him. (NRSV)

"Do not be alarmed" Now, why in the world or out of the world would this "young man" tell these women to not be alarmed? How could they not be alarmed? It's not every day that one speaks with angels. This would not be the most amazing part for the angels, and that's a different story that you can wait for in the narrative of the Gospel of Matthew's resurrection story.

The word "alarmed" comes from the Greek *ekthambeo*, meaning "utterly astounded," or maybe "greatly wondering." Other translations state the word "alarmed" to be "amazed." Alarmed means "to throw into terror or amazement" (Strong). This was how the women looked as they stood at a standstill, staring at the empty tomb with thoughts of "Maybe..." or "This is from bad to worse, He has been crucified, laid in a tomb, and now they have stolen His body, these grave robbers, with utter disrespect and depravity!" Whether it is "amazed" or "alarmed," I take liberty to think it was a mix of both and more!

The young man would say these important words: "He has risen." He would not say, "Your plans for Him as king have risen," or "Your understanding of Him has risen," or "Your circumstances have risen," or even "Your power, prestige, and possessions have risen." He would say, "Don't be terrified," and rightly so, for now their lives would truly be turned right side up, and they would follow the One through persecutions, unfairness, injustice, misunderstanding, misrepresentation, mistrial, and complete insecurity in the world.

And yet they would not be without Jesus ever again! All rules of nature changed; the dead will rise! The poor in spirit, the ones who mourn, the gentle, those who hunger and thirst for righteousness, the merciful, the pure in heart, the peacemakers, the ones persecuted for the sake of righteousness, the ones people will insult and persecute, yes, ALL of these shall be called blessed (Matt. 5:1–10). Truly, every valley shall be filled, every mountain will be brought low, the crooked will become straight, and the rough roads will be made smooth (Luke 3:5). The opposite of the world shall be made true—no wonder these women were terrified, amazed, shocked, and utterly astounded! I would be too! How about you?

> What in your life needs to be turned inside out, outside in, or wrong side up?

> Go to Jesus, look up and see He is risen, and believe—He will make that which is dead beautiful. *Selah.*

Jesus Christ—alarmingly and amazingly RISEN LORD!

Scene (Seen) 9

Tremors and Ecstasy

Mark 16:7-8

But go, tell his disciples and Peter that he is going ahead of you to Galilee; there you will see him, just as he told you. So, they went out and fled from the tomb, for terror and amazement had seized them; and they said nothing to anyone, for they were afraid. (*NRSV*)

Reread these verses, and then say what happened out loud.

Questions that will be raised through the devotion:
- So, what might be causing you tremors or ecstasy?
- How will you process this?
- **What might you think the women were thinking and feeling? Can you relate?**

*W*hy were these women afraid? They might have feared what they had seen; not every day does one see angels or men in dazzling clothing! They might have feared what they had heard. After all, Jesus' friends had denied Him, betrayed Him, or, at best, just stood by silently and cast Him down, with no controlling power to stop any of the madness of crucifying their beloved Jesus!

Why were they afraid? Were they afraid of His friends and the moment they would try to explain it to them? Were they afraid of their response to the words "Jesus is alive" and the men and their unbelief? Would they be afraid of more mockery? After all, women were not to be believed—at least in public. Would they be afraid of another moment when they would be reminded of how little their voice, their opinion, or their witness really mattered? Indeed, it would just be yet another time a woman was exaggerating!

"Trembling and astonishment"—the word is *tromos*, "with fear and trembling," used to describe the anxiety of one who completely distrusts his ability to meet all that is required, "but religiously does his utmost to fulfill his duty." (Strong, G5155). Does the word *tromos* sound familiar? Maybe "tremor" does. Have you ever stood in place, frozen by lead feet that keep you from escaping, terrified by the fact that you aren't confident in the least that you can do a task?

The question could be: Have you taken on a task larger than your abilities? Or is the question more along the lines that it was for these women: Have you been asked by God to take on a task way beyond what you want to do, or thought you were able to do? If it is the former, then expect the art of humility to come down your walk of life. If it is the latter, then your choice is to flee and be faced later with another ominous request from God or to stay, take a big gulp of courage, and step forward to learn the task of trusting an ALIVE Jesus.

Either way, as this writer sees it, there will be the painful goodness of humility or the tremoring goodness of trust nurtured, tested, and matured in the roots of your heart. Either way, following the alive Jesus will lead to a garden, and it might bring forth fruit despite your taking on too much or seeing yourself as too little. In both of these scenarios, the choice is to flee or stay the course. These women stayed the course!

These women, Mark would write, would say nothing, for they were afraid, but at least one of them would choose to go and tell the men, only to not be believed, and then proven completely accurate. The other Gospel writers will argue the point with Mark as to how many went to tell the disciples. But the point is: never you mind, for God prevails! Through tremors and through astonishment, *ekstasis*: "Any casting down of a thing from its proper place or state, displacement, a throwing of the mind out of its normal state, amazement, one who…is thrown into a state of blended fear and wonderment" (Strong, G1611). Ecstasy!

God prevails through tremors and ecstasy, through the one who "does his utmost to fulfill his or her duty."

Never you worry.

So—what might be causing you tremors or ecstasy?

How will you process this?

What might you think the women were thinking and feeling? Can you relate?

Can you see the Lord's goodness as He teaches you in the garden of your life and in your soul's circumstances?

Think about this through the day. Watch for those tremoring moments. Remember this.

Jesus Christ—Master Gardener!

Scene (Seen) 10

Love Beyond

Mark 16:7–13

But go, tell His disciples and Peter, "He is going ahead of you to Galilee; there you will see Him, just as He told you." They went out and fled from the tomb, for trembling and astonishment had gripped them; and they said nothing to anyone, for they were afraid. Now after He had risen early on the first day of the week, He first appeared to Mary Magdalene, from whom He had cast out seven demons. She went and reported to those who had been with Him, while they were mourning and weeping. When they heard that He was alive and had been seen by her, they refused to believe it. After that, He appeared in a different form to two of them while they were walking along on their way to the country. They went away and reported it to the others, but they did not believe them either.

Let's pause for a moment and learn some mechanics of Scripture. Starting with Mark 16:7, there are brackets around the rest of these written words. Why? The best manuscripts do not have these verses. It's just that simple. No hiding, no apology. They could have been added later. Some manuscripts contain these verses.

How was Scripture determined to be in the Bible, you might ask? Well, various manuscripts were copies of copies, sent from various places where the early church people were located. They would make copies, and those copies would be sent other places. Some of those places were considered more reputable in their scribal (writing) skills, and more consistent. This particular Scripture is in brackets, informing the reader that in some manuscripts, these words are not in the text. Either way, these particular words in Scripture don't take away from the risen Jesus story—but what they do add are some peculiar sightings by Mark. An early church father, Irenaeus, quoted from Mark 16:9–20. So there is some evidence these verses were part of Mark.

As a reminder, Mark, whose mother was Mary—yes, another Mary; it was a common name—was a young man who was mentored by Peter. The Jewish and Greek cultures looked highly on the system in which the young men were being discipled, or, in Greek terms, patronized. Peter was Mark's patron, the one he looked up to and learned from in his world—his very own walking and teaching university. Mark, in chapter sixteen, writes about Mary Magdalene as the one to whom Jesus first appeared, the one from whom Jesus had cast out seven demons. (Understanding that scholarship states that Mark's original text ends at verse eight, I would like permission to exercise imagination upon the rest of these verses in Mark 16, if only to ponder questions that the text raises for me, and for others who have read this great Gospel with me. Thank you, and so I proceed).

Now—when I ask my students if they know anything about Mary Magdalene, most of them mention her reputation as a prostitute, or they might be honest and tell me they saw her once in a movie called *The Da Vinci Code*, a conjecturing novel made into a box-office hit that is filled with delusional ideas, which conveyed her as having a relationship with Jesus.

So why do I rest on this verse about Mary Magdalene? Cultures haven't changed. Has the reader ever passed on news of another that was not our story to tell? Or can we attest to fake news circulating in these treacherous times, when we need truth? Exactly! Enough said on this topic; gossip destroys people, for nowhere in Scripture is Mary Magdalene aligned with sexual promiscuity.

Why is John Mark's the only Gospel to include this? Maybe later, as he heard stories, he wanted to set the church straight. Maybe Mary Magdalene was healed from seven demons, but we have no idea how she had been "possessed" by those seven demons—poor girl. Maybe the conjecture of "her sin" opening the door for demonic foul play was the purpose of these rumors. It reminds me of the story of the blind man being healed by Jesus in John 9, and how those around Jesus were asking, "Did this man sin, or did his parents?" Remember that story? Maybe it was someone else's sin in Mary's life that had been the real culprit for these torments of her tumultuous soul. What we do know from the wisdom of young John Mark, who had seen his patron (mentor), Peter, deny Jesus in a courtyard, was that no one is found without blemish, no one—not Mary, not John Mark, not Peter. Only one was without a big or small mess-up: Jesus! All were in need of a Savior who could relate to them in everything but were messing up or missing the mark (as in archery, when one misses the bullseye) in sin. Why do you and I (and maybe I am just speaking for myself) focus on the gossip or the seven demons, RATHER than on the words "whom He had cast out?"

No wonder Mary Magdalene was the first at the graveside of Jesus that morning; the women would join her later. He had healed her from the tremors of tomb life. Why wouldn't she go to serve her True Friend as He lay in His tomb? Oh, the sweet devotion and love of the Lord illustrated by the "least of these" in culture. Tongues may wag, and looks may be cast, but the ones who know where they have come from—the tombs of despair, the darkness of torture, the emptiness of self-serving—why, even the slanderers and gossips, they know where they have come from, and they know what Jesus had done for them. Jesus loved beyond scope or imagination. What have any of us done to receive love like this? A love that knows no speed limits, no borders, no walls, no boundaries, no rules, and no end; this is the love of Jesus. What did Mary have to lose? She announces to the disciples (the knowledgeable and fear-driven ones, including Peter) that she, Mary, had been with Him at the tomb. The fact is that even Peter "refused to believe it." Later, as we read in Mark 16:12–13, two others see Jesus and Peter, and their crowd will "not believe them either."

Could it be that John Mark is writing this, as he might even have helped Peter write the first two chapters of Peter? Mark wanted to bring to clarity that Jesus heals, Jesus died, Jesus is risen, and only Jesus is God. Mark wanted to make sure everyone who read his writings, from the very least—the youngest—to the woman who was healed of seven demons that they may know that Mary and her friends were the first honest truth-tellers; they had "been with Jesus."

Take time to be with Jesus, remember His healings and your needs, and let Him ask you the question: Have you diminished another person's character or made a list of offenses in your mind about another? Give these lists to Jesus and be with Him; He is alive and able to tell you to lay down your tremors, your doubts, your failures, your seeming successes, and your great treasures of life.

Then read Psalm 100.
    Shout
    Worship
    Come
    Know
    Enter

For the Lord is good, and His love endures forever; His faithfulness endures through all generations.

Jesus Christ—Faithful Savior.

Scene (Seen) 11
Flipping of Carts

Mark 16:12–13

After this he appeared in another form to two of them, as they were walking into the country. And they went back and told the rest, but they did not believe them. (*NRSV*)

My story: I was in the grocery store with my sons (three of them, at the time) and their cousins—five little boys, ages two to six years old. What was I thinking? My two-year-old was sitting in the front of the grocery cart I was pushing. The other boys were walking, skipping, and running alongside the cart. David, my four-year-old, came running up and jumped on the bottom rail of the cart, and it tilted a little, so I stopped and said, "David, don't do that, because you could tip the cart." We proceeded down the aisle. I forgot to grab some cereal from the adjacent aisle, so I said, "You all stay here and I'll be right back; I forgot cereal." My bad!

My first mistake was leaving the cart and telling little boys to stay there! Never do that! I was only away for a second, running around the corner to get the cereal, but as I reached for the box, I heard a crash and a scream. I ran back around to see the cart, with my two-year-old in it, completely overturned, with the end of the cart pointing toward the ceiling and the front railing of the cart resting on the floor. My two-year-old was terrorized and holding on for dear life, staring at the floor. Thank the good Lord that his knees were tucked under and not straight out, or they would not have been a pretty sight under the weight of the cart handle, as the cart looked like a child's rocket ship waiting to take off.

Flipping of Carts

Adrenaline rushing, I lifted up the cart, handle and all, while holding my boy, Daniel, and consoling him. Yes, count me as THAT mom. I mean, I tried—I still try—but honestly, now having four sons, I can tell you that I had to learn. They were the school I went to each day: the school of mothering boys! It was all I could do not to start bawling my eyes out, but I had to stay composed, so as I held my baby close to my heart and comforted him, I looked up and down that aisle, and no boy was in sight.

After getting my son quieted, I went to look for the boys, placing my son in the larger part of the cart, as he would have nothing to do with the seat. I didn't blame him; neither would I! I found the boys cowering in the next aisle. People were looking, so I needed to just calmly get them, get our groceries, and get out. I told the boys, "Mommy shouldn't have left the basket, but who jumped on it?" No one would say; that's a given at any age. Clearly, they were a well-formed union with one thought in their minds: "Let's be good, we promise."

So I said, "Let's just leave; I'm done. And by the way, no treats." There wasn't even a groan from the union members. As I pushed the cart, with Daniel sitting in the main basket part and looking on with terror, my David, forgetting the last ten minutes completely, ran around the cart and jumped on the end to hitch a ride. Now, he was a thinly built little four-year-old boy, but with just the right momentum, he had jumped, and the cart started to tip over toward him. I know you think I am making this up. I promise you I am not. The cart started to tip, only this time—, yes, this time, I had my hands on the cart handle (like any normal, responsible mother), and as my part of the cart raised from the floor, I was in control.

Poor Daniel—the one who'd had enough of grocery carts for one day, to say the least—grabbed the sides of the cart, with determination in his eyes. It was the look of a little brother who had two older brothers, a "fool me once, shame on you; fool me twice, shame on me" kind of look, only he was just two, so there was also terror at the thought that this time, he was going to be catapulted out. No worries, I had the handle, and in half a second, I brought the handle part of the cart down with a solid thud. Everyone was safe—EXCEPT for my shin.

I brought the cart right down on my shin. I literally saw stars—not kids, but stars. I was bent over, still holding the war-zone cart and fighting back tears, with all of the boys silently staring and probably pondering, "What is she going to do?" Smart question! I caught my breath, collected my painful stars, and said, "Let's get out of here NOW!" They were quiet, and walked behind me in single file, not saying a word as I carried Daniel out of the store, limping. As we walked past the pharmacy section, my oldest said, "Mom, look, they have canes. Maybe we should buy one for you." More like maybe I could trade them for a cane!

The people in the store were all admiring those "cute little boys, all in a line," and probably wondering what happened to that crippled mother. People in grocery stores never know the whole story, and always make judgments! We drove home. I fed them silently and made everyone take a nap whether they were tired or not.

As I tell this story, no one really gets the fullness of my words. Why would I share this story?

In Mark 16:14–17, Jesus finally shows up. He knows that Mary Magdalene and the other women have told the story of their lives being turned upside down like a kid in a grocery store cart, and yet no one else would believe either of them!

> **Have you ever had what I call a grocery-cart-tipping moment in your life, when all that is of value gets emptied upside down and you find yourself alone, just trying to scramble, pick up those valuable pieces of your life, and tip the cart of your life back upright? Write about it, or just think it through if you are not a writer. Then think about that moment and the times when you tried to share the significance of it, and no one really believed you or even really cared. How might that make you feel or think?**

As you share your story because you need to process, have you ever had the experience of people who are listening just wanting to "continue as normal?" Or have you met people that listen to you for a second and then talk about what's on their minds, or pat you on the head and say, "Yeah, right—I think you might just be exaggerating a bit, getting a bit worked up, so just settle down and everything will be fine."

If that's the case, I'm sorry. Find a true friend who will validate you; that friend is real. Find a true friend who will just listen and sit and help you process your thoughts, your confusions, and your crazy feelings, and then rest with you.

No matter what, Jesus reminds us, there really is only One who will truly get it; after all, His Father watched the whole story: yours and His.

This is what Mary Magdalene, the other women, and Cleopas and his unnamed companion were experiencing. No one believed them.

> What's your story—your grocery-cart-tipping story that no one would believe? Write it out if that helps, or just go take a walk and say it out loud to God; He's listening, and He is really ALIVE.

Jesus Christ—Steady GOD in the Turmoil!

Scene (Seen) 12

Foxhole of Rebuke

Mark 16:14–16

Later he appeared to the eleven themselves as they were sitting at the table; and he upbraided them for their lack of faith and stubbornness, because they had not believed those who saw him after he had risen. And he said to them, "Go into all the world and proclaim the good news to the whole creation. The one who believes and is baptized will be saved; but the one who does not believe will be condemned." (*NRSV*)

Jesus rebuked them. "Rebuke" is not a fluffy word or a soft discussion. "Rebuke" means to disapprove in a harsh and critical manner, straight to the point, no holding back. How are you and I with criticism? Are you and I defensive at disapproval from a friend? Jesus was their true Friend. I wonder how John Mark took it? He had to be there, listening and watching as the older guys were looking on, astounded, disbelieving, and utterly speechless. First, Jesus was in front of them—shocker! If that was not enough, He didn't come knocking meekly at the door; He appeared to them. "Too much," you say or think? Me too! Wait, so you are telling me that Jesus appeared to the eleven-plus men, and his first words were a rebuke? Wow. "Rebuked" or "reproached," in the language of John Mark, meant "upbraided, reviled, cut in one's teeth, to defame" (Strong, G3679).

There are very few places in Scripture where Jesus rebukes His friends. He will rebuke others who are high in authority in that culture; He rebukes the demons; He rebukes the winds—but only

Foxhole of Rebuke

in a few places does He rebuke His friends. They might have felt a bit rebuked when they were walking with Jesus one day, arguing who would be the greatest and who would serve whom (Luke 22:24–27). They might have at least felt foolish when they rebuked Jesus for receiving little children and holding them—after all, Jesus was important (Matt. 19:13)—or when Peter told Jesus what he, Peter, wasn't going to allow Jesus to do! Mark surely remembered that incident, since Mark was always watching and learning from his hero, Peter! "But turning around and seeing His disciples, He **rebuked** Peter and said, 'Get behind Me, Satan; for you are not setting your mind on God's interests, but man's'" (Mark 8:33).

Why does Jesus rebuke them? The words aren't recorded; I wonder if it was too much for John Mark to write. Nevertheless, Mark does write the reason for the rebuke, so he got the message clearly: "He reproached them for their unbelief and hardness of heart; because they had not believed those who had seen Him after He had risen" (Mark 16:14). Unbelief means "destitution of spiritual perceptions—*skleros kardia*" (Strong, G4641), which means "hardness of heart;" it's where we get our word "scoliosis" (curvature of the spine). *Kardia* means heart—our word "cardiac" comes from it. The heart was considered by the Jews to be the core, unlike our culture, which dismisses the heart and considers it to be the emotions. The Jews paid attention to the core: the heart. Jesus is severely reprimanding them for not believing their friends. He is rebuking them for the curvature of their hearts!

There is a gentleman by the name of Tony Campolo who has been an advocate for youth for forty years. One day I was listening to a speech he was giving, and I will never forget the example he gave us. He spoke of the purpose and the dangers of foxholes in World War I. Foxholes were places of protection, but when the enemy entered the foxholes, shooting would begin, and sometimes soldiers on the same side would accidentally be shot by their comrades, thus the term "friendly fire." The word, "friendly," was used because it was from the same side in the foxhole, and a kindred soldier would be mortally shot. As Mr. Campolo was speaking, he paused and then shouted, "Christian church—the enemy is out there," and he pointed out.

I would never forget it. It was a rebuke—a very strong rebuke. The heart of his message was that those who follow Jesus are just like the new believers Jesus is rebuking in this story—they dice, chop, and cut at one another. Christians don't believe in one another, when TRUTH is essential for life, but have hardness of heart toward one another. Just like those disciples, they—rather, WE—don't believe each other's stories. We are so busy deconstructing everything, in the hope of discovering something ourselves, that we push away our fellow followers of Jesus. We criticize, we refuse to listen, and we communicate what we hear, not for the purpose of progress for the other. Oh, this is hard to write, but I have been encouraged and then flipped the coin of my own actions and heart, and have come up with the empty pockets of "I've got nothing, Lord—You are right."

Notice that the disciples were reclining, kicking back and enjoying a meal. Way to be a downer, Jesus—I mean, come on, wouldn't you, if you were Jesus, come running in with hugs and kisses, crying with joy to know you were alive and could be with your friends? I sure would have, but then again, remember, I have empty pockets because I have not believed my friends many times. I have fought to be the greatest, and like Peter, I have definitely told Jesus what to do, and have not wanted to sign up for anything that made me feel remotely uncomfortable. Well, maybe that's a bit too much, but I think we often want to skim the surface and move into the fluffy Jesus love.

Charles Spurgeon, a pastor quoted in an earlier section of this book, writes about Psalm 36 and the one who doesn't want to receive the rebukes of God. This person, who lacks the ability to receive criticism from a brother, puffs himself up. Spurgeon writes:

> God-fearing men see their sins and bewail them, where the reverse is the case, we may be sure there is no fear of God. *"He flattereth himself in his own eyes."* He counts himself a fine

fellow, worthy of great respect. He quiets his conscience, and so deceives his own judgment as to reckon himself a pattern of excellence; if not for morality, yet for having sense enough not to be enslaved by rules which are bonds to others. He is the free thinker, the man of strong mind, the hater of can't, the philosopher; and the servants of God are, in his esteem, mean-spirited and narrow-minded. Of all flatteries this is the most absurd and dangerous. (Spurgeon)

The one who does not receive the hard teachings of Jesus flatters him or herself unto danger. This was one of the harshest moments that Jesus was recorded as having with His close friends. Their choice was to argue back, get mad, or leave the room—freeze, fight, or flight.

> Will I let Jesus remind me, and will you let Jesus remind you, of the times we have refused to believe our sister or brother in Christ? Will we listen to their story long enough to understand them, and maybe even see then their perspective? Are we so preoccupied with our own selfish lives that we refuse to listen and receive what they have to say?
>
> You may not agree with them, but did they leave you feeling validated, loved, and whole, or did they leave you feeling rejected? Is this what you or I want?
>
> Humility is listening and bending into the position of saying, "I'm sorry, please forgive me."

Are you and I critical of our teammates? Are you and I having discussions with others about them and building our palaces of power, rather than discussing them with GOD? In other words, do I talk about my friends to others or to GOD?

Or, on the flipside, maybe you have felt rejected by believers.

> Do you think this has slipped the notice of an infinite God? Maybe God wants you to wait upon Him, trust in Him to look past your hurt and pain, and forgive?

Either way, God wants you and me to learn from His friend, whom He rebuked. This is an opportunity to learn to be either unbelieving or believing, hard-hearted or soft-hearted; **how will we respond?**

> **Take some time to reflect on this. Wherever you are in this, Jesus is risen—will you let Him rise up in your sister's or brother's heart?**

That means there must be space for Him to move in them, spaces of failure and spaces of short-sightedness. **Will you and I behave the same way or make room for Jesus to change those around us?**

Unity in the body of believers requires space, belief in the Christ and one another, and diligent hearts to listen and receive. Then, and only then, will Jesus' words in Mark 16:15–18 come to pass:

> And He said to them, "Go into all the world and preach the gospel to all creation. He who has believed and has been baptized shall be saved; but he who has disbelieved shall be condemned. These signs will accompany those who have believed: in My name they will cast out demons, they will speak with new tongues; they will pick up serpents, and if they drink any deadly *poison*, it will not hurt them; they will lay hands on the sick, and they will recover."

HEALING FOR THE WORLD!

> **Take time now to stop. Breathe in, and be mindful of your own thoughts, the tension in your neck or your feeling of wanting to get up and leave. Remember—breath is how God created and creates anew.**
>
> **Breathe out: Christ is risen.**
>
> **Breathe in: be aware of moments of impatience with those in your life, when you are not willing to listen and give space.**

Breathe out: Christ is risen.

Breathe in: check your heart for bitterness.

Breathe out: Christ is risen, and repent—this means to turn around in your thinking, your heart, and your actions.

Breathe in and breathe out: Christ is risen indeed.

Jesus Christ—FOREVER TRUTH!

Scene (Seen) 13

Word and Deed, Indeed!

Mark 16:17–20

And these signs will accompany those who believe: by using my name they will cast out demons; they will speak in new tongues; they will pick up snakes in their hands, and if they drink any deadly thing, it will not hurt them; they will lay their hands on the sick, and they will recover." (*NRSV*)

I know Scene (Seen) 12 was difficult. I have been allowing others to challenge me in regard to truth and communication. I have a small group—well, actually, a medium group—of young professional women, and they challenge me all the time. I am so thankful for them in my life. I think I learn from them more than they learn from me! They are teachers, nurses, graphic designers, realtors, event coordinators, and on and on. Each one has a story, and we are keen to listen to, encourage, and exhort one another. We are from different political parties; we are from different cultures; we are each unique on the enneagram chart; we have different callings; yet we have kindred hearts, and we applaud and comfort one another. I am so thankful for them because I want to learn, and learning only happens when I go against my own grain and comfort zones, and listen outside of my box. I write this to encourage you to be learners for life; it is good.

Going against his own comfort zones, the follower of Jesus, John Mark, had been on a steep learning curve with his mentor Peter and the rest of the disciples, discovering this Jesus and who He really was: God's Son. Mark was writing this, continuing in his

Word and Deed, Indeed!

"so then this happened" manner of seeing and writing about their lives while following Jesus. "So then, when the Lord Jesus had spoken to them, He was received into heaven and sat down at the right hand of God."

Mark takes his breath. Maybe this breath was important for Mark. Whether he wrote this section later or it was there from the beginning as he labored over the manuscripts, it's as if Mark is looking back on all of their adventures, including a possible moment in his life when Jesus and the rest were at the garden the night Jesus would be arrested. Mark might have even heard about the coming arrest and run to warn Peter, Jesus, and the rest about the coming disaster for Jesus, when Judas would show the temple guards where Jesus would be. Maybe, just maybe, Mark would have known about the arrest. Was he the young man that only he himself writes about in this verse: "A young man was following Him, wearing nothing but a linen sheet over his naked body; and they seized him. But he pulled free of the linen sheet and escaped naked" (Mark 14:51–52)?

Another adventure he might have been thinking about as he penned this sweet and swift Gospel was the one he would have years after Jesus had left the earth. Mark had gone with his cousin, Barnabas, who asked Mark to accompany him and Paul on their first missionary journey. Or maybe Mark was thinking about the adventure in which he left Paul and Barnabas in the middle of Pamphylia.

According to Gene Edwards, both Paul and Barnabas would be deeply grieved that John Mark left them: "Paul was not angry with Mark, but he was sorry to hear his request. Finally, he and Barnabas capitulated to Mark's desires, though they desperately needed him. What coursed through Paul's mind, however, was concern for what it would do to Mark's inner man if he turned back. Paul feared that Mark would never trust himself again if he returned to Jerusalem" (Edwards, 55–56).

Whether it was the marathon—that the youth just couldn't keep up with Paul—or ill health, or homesickness, the bottom line was that Mark would leave him. Was he reflecting on this as he wrote those final words of his, "And they promptly reported all these instructions to Peter and his companions. And after that, Jesus Himself sent out through them from east to west the sacred and imperishable proclamation of eternal salvation?"

Or was Mark thinking about the next adventure, when Paul refused to take him along again but Barnabas fought for him? Barnabas and Paul would split. Paul would take Silas and head northwest, and Barnabas would take Mark and head southwest; God works good in the middle of conflicting times. Mark, as tradition has it, would be a leader in Alexandria, and would later be martyred in 68 AD. All of this is to say that Mark would be reflecting back on all of his adventures in Christ, and then he wrote his own "Great Commission."

By the way, Matthew wasn't the only owner of the only Great Commission in Matthew 28! Mark would write, "Go into all the world and preach the gospel in all creation" (Mark 16:15). I'm sure he was thinking about preaching the good news to the young, to the old, to the successful, to those who fail, to the rich and the poor, to the northerners, the southerners, the easterners, and the westerners. It's as if Mark's youth was still showing up. "Go into the WHOLE WIDE WORLD and preach the gospel IN THE WHOLE WIDE CREATION!" Can you imagine a little boy saying this, with arms motioning widely, in a demonstrative, loud, and boldly spoken proclamation? He would write that power followed that preaching: casting out demons, speaking new tongues, picking up serpents (i.e., Paul in Malta, being bitten by a poisonous viper and not even being affected, in Acts 28:3), drinking deadly poison (who knows what adventure that was!), laying hands on the sick and healing them. John Mark says there will be actions that follow salvation.

After writing all this, Mark breathes and writes his last "so then." Mark, the author of the Gospel of Interruptions. He knew this lesson well: some of life's interruptions are left unfinished and untold. I don't know why in my lifetime, and neither will you, and neither did Mark.

Word and Deed, Indeed!

BUT notice what John Mark knew to be positively true: "And they went out and preached everywhere, while the Lord worked with them and confirmed the word by the signs that followed." Mark was convinced. It was not them BUT CHRIST. Christ before them, Christ behind them, Christ in them, Christ above them and below them—Christ. "And they promptly reported all these instructions to Peter and his companions. And after that, Jesus Himself sent out through them from east to west the sacred and imperishable proclamation of eternal salvation" (Mark 16:19).

All may be helpless, and for sure, those of us in this 2020 vision year have felt the despair of helplessness! All may be helpless, yes, and hopeless, but in Christ we can serve and help. The truth is that in Christ we can be HOPEFUL in the middle of the interruptions, which can be left in the hands of the Father, worked out in the strength of Jesus Christ, and breathed into us by the Spirit of God. Truth is: in Christ we can be redeemed (bought back with His life), restored (as His resurrected body has been made alive), and renewed. Amen.

Jesus Christ—God the Ultimate Adventurer!

"Christ with me,
Christ before me,
Christ behind me,
Christ in me,
Christ beneath me,
Christ above me,
Christ on my right,
Christ on my left,
Christ when I lie down,
Christ when I sit down,
Christ when I arise,
Christ in the heart of every man who thinks of me,
Christ in the mouth of everyone who speaks of me,
Christ in every eye that sees me,
Christ in every ear that hears me." (Saint Patrick)

Scene (Seen) 14

The Wonder of First Fruits

Matthew 28:1

After the Sabbath, as the first day of the week was dawning, Mary Magdalene and the other Mary went to see the tomb. And suddenly there was a great earthquake, for an angel of the Lord, descending from heaven, came and rolled back the stone and sat on it. (*NRSV*)

Reread these verses, and then say what happened out loud. Questions that will be raised through the devotion:
- **What now do you understand to be the significance of the First Fruits Feast?**
- **What have you believed to be dead in your life: dreams, hopes, cares, desires?**

The Gospel writer Matthew was a tax collector who made a living at the expense of his community; "A little for you, a little for me" might have been his motto. The Romans collected taxes; the Pharisees collected money for the temple; it seemed like everyone was always taking money!

Matthew was no exception, as he might have charged his community a "little extra" for his time and effort. After all, he deserved it, right? He was working hard, and his friends wouldn't miss the extra shekel! His reasonings were as many as the coins: everyone knows, who cares, others do other things; steal from the rich and give to the poor! This Gospel writer cared about the details of the day; his life's job accounted for this. Matthew's main mistake would be failing to consider that omission was as critical as commission, except when it came to his own selfish gain. Matthew would easily look away as he slipped money to himself under the table—call it "charging the community more than the Romans want" so that he could make a little money. After all, he wasn't like the zealots running around and destroying everything, and he definitely wasn't into enforcing the rules, like the Pharisees!

And yet here, in these verses, Matthew is significantly changed by following the Son of God, God with us, Son of Man, writing an outrageous story about resurrection and the Feast of First Fruits. Matthew knew a little secret that really isn't much of a secret, except for those who have an innate desire to "fix" things, people, structures, or even agendas (as we shall see later in the devotions). The bottom line was: Matthew knew HE WASN'T THE SAVIOR. Do we know this principle? Mark seems to be the Gospel of Interruptions. Luke seems to be the Gospel about the Servant Savior. And now Matthew seems to be the loud and clear Gospel that all are in need of a Savior—the Messiah.

After the Passover and the Sabbath that morning, at dawn, the high priest would make his way through the sleepy town to the nearest farmland. He would scope out that early morning, looking for the first evidence of new growth and new life, and with joy in his reach he would scoop up (roots and all) that baby sprig of a barley shoot in his hands, like a proud father scooping up his infant son. **He would raise it up high to Jehovah, the Father of the heavenlies** (how ironic when you think of what's happening on the other side of Jerusalem, where the One would have risen from the ground—the tomb), and sing to God's glory. Then, with plant in hand, the high priest would go back to the temple, and there the city would begin the celebration of First Fruits—the celebration that there would be a crop, and all would be well. This had been practiced for hundreds of years, and now, this day, it would become the spiritual journey of all the followers of Jesus. Matthew would have known this; he was Jewish. It was important, the day after Sabbath, after Passover; it was a day to look forward to, a day to expect new beginnings—new crops.

Sincerely SEEN

At the dawn of a new beginning, we might all want to look toward something rather than looking back. Mary Magdalene and the "other Mary" were no exception. They were trying with all their hearts to look toward something during those dawning hours.

> "Now after the Sabbath, as it began to dawn toward the first *day* of the week, Mary Magdalene and the other Mary came to look at the grave" (Matt. 28:1–2).

Why, on this blessed beginning-of-earth day, would two women be going to "look at the grave?" It might have been that they were coming out of the shock of the events after Passover on that infamous day when Jesus Christ of Nazareth was executed, and they just wanted to go where their best Friend lay. It might have been that they were women of conscience who remembered that their best Friend had not been given a proper burial, so they went to accomplish the task of anointing his body. Matthew writes, "Going to look at the grave." He understood their hearts like anyone who has lost a loved one would; they were going to look to reaffirm their shocking and disillusioned thoughts; Jesus was dead. Maybe they went to look at the grave with the hope that even sitting by the dead body of Jesus would bring their hearts comfort. For as you know, Jesus was always good about bringing comfort in a chaotic crisis.

> "And behold, a severe earthquake had occurred, for an angel of the Lord descended from heaven and came and rolled away the stone and sat upon it" (Matt. 28:2).

Later, the women would tell Matthew and the other disciples what they experienced on the dawn of First Fruits. They experienced an earthquake. It seemed, on that dawning day, to bring doom and more trouble. How could things get worse? Neither had been able to sleep well that night. The haunting, horrid memories of their King of Kings being crucified kept them from restful sleep. They arose early and quietly slipped through town to look at His grave while the priest was headed to the barley field.

When it seemed that things could not get worse, they did; a severe earthquake occurred. Have you ever been in an earthquake before? Maybe not physically, but mentally? I have been in a few physical earthquakes, having lived south of Mexico City. It's always a deep shake-up (no pun intended) when the ground you think is stable shakes beneath your feet. It is unnerving to feel the foundations of your life grumbling and rumbling under your feet, under your house, or under you, period! Foundations are supposed to be strong, firm, stable, and unmoving. Earthquakes cause those who live through them to wait for the aftershocks and realize that nothing is stable under the heavens. If I had been there, or maybe if you had been, I would have cried out with the utmost of passion, "What more God? What more can happen?"

What do you do when things go from bad to worse? What do you do when your life foundations seem to shake beneath you and bring you face-to-face with your doubts? Do you yell or silently withdraw? Do you rant or inwardly die in your heart, sitting down to quit and giving into depression?

They had no time to struggle through these seismic "shocking's" of soul and spirit! "For an angel of the Lord descended from heaven and rolled away the stone and sat upon it." Are you hearing the heavenly trumpet blasts, bragging about God's most outlandish feat yet? The "Dun Ta Ta Daaaa" kind of trumpet blast that pronounces the grandest of kingly processions possible; the RESURRECTION OF THE SON OF MAN is being presented. I can just hear the heavenly trumpets proudly and resolutely proclaiming: "Jesus is not here." This was Matthew's rendition of what the women experienced. He wrote in an almost matter-of-fact fashion, something an accountant of his reputation would do, and something those telling the truth seem to do when they record the details. God's angel came out of heaven, "rolled back the stone, and sat upon it."

I imagine, at this point, for Mary Magdalene and the other Mary, time seemed to have stopped, and everything moved in a slow-motion manner. Whether they saw the angel descend from heaven or not, one thing is certain: the angel sat victoriously on that stone, and no one could deny the reason why the angel took such a seat on that day! In that culture, sitting was often a position of grief. But not on this First Fruits morning!

On this dawn toward the first day of the week, while the priest was raising his hands to God in thanks for first fruits, God raised His hand, emptied the tomb of His only begotten Son, and posted His own holy guard to proclaim this First of the First Fruits news to a couple of women who had gone to look at the dead. This was not what they expected. God showed up when they least expected. What they expected was death, and what they experienced was the shaking of the foundations of their lives, raising their eyes to see the heralding angel victoriously sitting on the tomb's door, which humans had thought would hold down Jesus. NO TOMB, NO GROUND, NO EARTHEN VESSEL CAN RESTRAIN THE SON OF GOD.

The women were to learn the good news, the angel triumphantly sat on that hewn rock, and the proclamation of First Fruits Day was their own now. A few years later, Paul, an apostle of Jesus, would pen these words to the Corinthians, a culture that valued possessions, people, and power: "But now Christ has been raised from the dead, the **first fruits** of those who are asleep."

Jesus Christ is the FIRST FRUIT of the Dead.

Questions:

What do you now understand to be the significance of the First Fruits Feast?

What have you believed to be dead in your life: dreams, hopes, cares, desires?

Can you imagine yourself walking to that tomb with friends and seeing how God might roll away the stone?

What are you looking forward to in your life? How might Scripture change your perspective in looking forward?

How does this Scripture bring you hope?

Scene (Seen) 15

Come and See

Matt. 28:3–7

His appearance was like lightning, and his clothing white as snow. For fear of him the guards shook and became like dead men. But the angel said to the women, "Do not be afraid; I know that you are looking for Jesus who was crucified. He is not here; for he has been raised, as he said. Come, see the place where he lay. Then go quickly and tell his disciples, 'He has been raised from the dead, and indeed he is going ahead of you to Galilee; there you will see him.' This is my message for you." (*NRSV*)

Are the Roman guards shaking because of their fear of the severe earthquake or their fear of the angel? Would you be shaking? Maybe some of you reading this are shaking in your anxiety about life's earthquakes or the startling realization that there is a spiritual world, and you don't know what to think about it. No judgment here, just questions that I have asked myself as I have slowly read these verses. What are you thinking?

*A*ctually, these Roman guards would be like modern day marine corps specialists. These guards had one objective in their mission: to guard this one-manned—or rather, one Son-of-Manned—gravesite so that no one tampered with or removed the body of this mysterious man who claimed to be God. It was either that or to give their own lives for this Jesus of Nazareth's body if it was stolen! These guards were not only trained but intensely feared, and yet they shook and became like dead men, stilled by this unbelievably powerful moment.

The startling part of this story is not really that these soldiers were silenced and frozen with fear. Anyone who has ever experienced true fear knows the sensation: palms sweaty, mind racing to flee, heart beating so loud you can hear it, overtaken with such a flood of feelings that all you can do is freeze—even men who have fought battles! They become like dead men, and one would think the angel would settle their nerves, for after all, men were highly valued, especially powerful Roman men. Either that or wipe them out!

But not this time. Time stood still as the angel spoke to the women. This would be highly frowned upon in that culture; women were not to be spoken to in public—they had no rights, and were to serve and be silent. The angel, Matthew records, never even turned to the powerful men; it was as if he had been sent for the looked-over, the insignificant, the ones society considered weak. Again—God makes a statement, as He did years before, when Jesus taught on a mountaintop:

> Blessed are the poor in spirit, for theirs is the kingdom of heaven. Blessed are those who mourn, for they shall be comforted. Blessed are the gentle, for they shall inherit the earth. Blessed are those who hunger and thirst for righteousness, for they shall be satisfied. Blessed are the merciful, for they shall receive mercy. Blessed are the pure in heart, for they shall see God. Blessed are the peacemakers, for they shall be called sons of God. Blessed are those who have been persecuted for the sake of righteousness, for theirs is the kingdom of heaven. (Matt. 5:3–10)

Jesus is always for the ones who are poor in spirit, who mourn, who are gentle. Always for the "little people," as Dale Bruner would translate "the gentle." Those who served Jesus, the angels, knew His agenda, and it was overwhelming to them! It was as if the news around heaven was that women came looking for Jesus, who had been crucified. It was truth! The Son of Man crucified, fully man, fully dead. Did the angel look with fondness at these courageous women who would risk their lives, drop their reputations, and be known as followers of the criminal in order to see and anoint His dead body, out of respect for and grieving the loss of their Friend?

And then came the glorious words, not sung in celestial symphony, as when Jesus' glorious birth was announced, but spoken in clarity, precisely the moment after the severe earthquake. First comes the shake-up of normal life and then comes the shock. Not the aftershock of an earthquake but the aftershock of these words: "He is not here, He is risen, just as He said" (Matt. 28:5).

These words pierced their minds and perceptions, shook the core of what is real, and turned their grievous day inside out, into a glorious day, yet not without trial. Jesus is the Savior, no need to stress. Oh, that you and I could have been at that garden tomb on that clear day to hear these words: "He is not here, He is risen" (Matt. 28:5). Would we be different?

The angel spoke to the women words of comfort, "Do not be afraid" (Matt. 28:5), and words of a power unknown before or since this infamous resurrection day. They had the courage to look for their dead King, and they were told: "Come and see where He was lying. Go quickly and tell His disciples that He has risen from the dead" (Matt. 28:6). It wasn't that the angel spoke with a booming voice; it was that all creation was hanging in the silence. The manly Roman power was silenced, the birds were silenced by the earthquake, and the ground was silenced from its shaking, so that the words of that Good News angel seemed to echo in the canyons of heaven. God invites: "Come and see."

Hearing those words would be like hearing the earth-shattering silence and whispering truths of life, piercing the air as they are spoken. Words like: "You have a son," or "She has cancer," or "Your father was found dead," or "Will you marry me," or "I want a divorce," or "We want your resignation," or "You are hired." These are the kind of word truths we either want to hear or don't want to hear. They are like the words spoken to those women by the angel.

Experiences and other people have a way of pressing into our lives at moments like these. You know, they are the experiences that you feel least ready for and least qualified to endure. I was the first female Biblical professor hired to teach Biblical studies at my amazing university. I didn't know that at the time, but I would find out on the first day, while filling out the paperwork. I don't like pioneering, but it seems that in life, there will always be tasks created for such a time for each of us to learn—how not to rely upon ourselves or hide but to trust in the Lord. This was that time for me, and I told myself it would be okay, no big deal; just press on and try not to look awkward. Yeah, right! It was my first real day of teaching an Old Testament class. A student raised his hand as I began to teach, and said, "Professor Mason, may I ask you a question?"

"Why, of course," I replied, "Ask away." The student then said, "Why is it that only men wrote the Bible?" The class became icily quiet. There was an awkward silence, and in my mind, I prayed, "God, this is NOT happening right now; it's the first day of classes! I know I'm a woman teaching men and women, but why is he asking me here, right now?"

I imagined the silence in the garden that early resurrection morning, when Mary Magdalene and the other Mary came to look at the grave. They didn't want to be noticed; they wanted to fly under the radar, like so many others I know—undocumented people, people who owe rent money, people in need, and people who seem less than the norm, whatever the norm is in the prominent culture. The women in the garden just wanted to work and live without fear, in community, living and celebrating life. They just wanted to be near their Friend and give due respect to the dead. I can relate. Can you relate?

Going back to class that day, I waited silently, and then answered the young college man, "I don't know why it was only men, but I sure am glad those men wrote the Scriptures; God's

Come and See

Word is magnificent!" More awkward silence followed, and my heart was pounding as I tried to go back to my planned lesson on Genesis 2 about being created in God's image, male and female. The silence deepened, and right then, this resurrection story popped into my head, and I raised a question.

"Now, let me ask you a question," I said, calling out his name. The student shifted in his seat as he replied confidently, seeming to gloat about his question, which posed doubts in his colleagues' minds as to whether or not it was right for me to be teaching Scripture in a higher institute of learning.

"Sure, go for it," he replied. (By the way, I don't think I ever had the nerve to give my professors permission to talk, but it's a different culture, and I'm not cancelling it. I rather love the challenge of engaging this new culture.) I turned and looked at him in the same way, I am sure, that the women at that tomb went in to look and see: courageously but cautiously.

"I do not know why only men wrote the Scriptures, but why is it that only women showed up first at the Lord's tomb, and were commanded to come and see where He was lying, and then were commanded to go tell the disciples He had risen from the dead?"

The class paused for "a minute" to think through the significance of what I asked, and then there was an eruption of shouts and a "whoa," and I had officially earned the right to be heard! Relaxation came with the understanding that maybe, just maybe, I might be okay for that postmillennial generation to listen to in class. I was relieved that the Lord had reminded me of the resurrection story at that moment, as I taught Genesis 1–2, that both male and female were made in God's image to be used by the King of Kings to bring Him glory. That resurrection day, women showed up first, and men wrote about them showing up first—resurrection beauty! Just as that day in class was a "drop-the-microphone" day for me and those students, so I believe it took only one moment for the silence at the grave of the dead Jesus to be recognized as empty indeed. Then the celebration of all creation must have exploded into the clearest of symphonies, on that First Fruits Feast Day! Indeed, Jesus was and IS alive; He conquered death and all odds of being ONLY man. He is NOT only Fully Man, but He is FULLY GOD, now, today, tomorrow, and forever.

Indeed, the angel who descended and rolled away that stone did absolutely nothing to release Jesus from the tomb; he was just created to bring part of this glorious story of new creation to God's image bearers. Jesus was already raised. He just let the angel proclaim the most REAL news on the face of earth for eternity: "Jesus is not here, He has been raised from the dead."

And by the way, that student and I became a great united team, helping others in the class to know and follow the God who raised Jesus Christ from the dead—who had women at the tomb to witness this first, and then had men write about it! What a great experience, to learn from one another!

> What impossible situations are you experiencing? What would be a "drop the mic" moment for you right now?
>
> How could this news of Jesus beating death be instrumental in your life right now?
>
> Reread Matthew 5 and then reimagine the angel saying, "Come and see." Then imagine entering that empty tomb. Ask the Lord for vision for yourself and others. Ask the Lord for a new expectancy for Him in your own heart.

Jesus Christ is Fully God!

Scene (Seen) 16

Bookends of Beholding Grace!

Matthew 28:7–8

Then go quickly and tell his disciples, "He has been raised from the dead, and indeed he is going ahead of you to Galilee; there you will see him. This is my message for you." So they left the tomb quickly with fear and great joy, and ran to tell his disciples. (*NRSV*)

Tax collector Matthew is methodical and linear in his written work of Gospel truth. According to the *NRSV* translation, Matthew writes the word "indeed he is going." But what is being communicated here is much clearer in the New American Standard Bible, "And go quickly and tell His disciples that He has risen from the dead; and behold, He is going ahead of you to Galilee. There you will see Him; behold, I have told you." Matthew, twice repeats the word "behold" in the words of the angel to the women. Actually, he will use the word "behold" over forty-four times in his recorded story of Jesus. "Behold," I think, is one of Matthew's favorite commands throughout his written words of hope: This word, "behold" translated in the original language of Greek, is *idou which means* to behold, see, perceive with your mind, pay attention (Strongs, G2400). The angel is wanting the disciples to pay attention to something profound after the word "behold." This word is actually written in the command form, meaning there was no choice or "pay attention!" Let's process what that might be.

Matthew bookends this part of the angelic instructions. Why doesn't he write "behold" or "indeed" when he states that Jesus is risen from the dead? Could it be that the resurrection of Jesus was not the most difficult part of the news for this angel messenger to declare? After all, heaven knew that earth could not contain the Maker of earth; earth could, and still can, be held in place only by the Maker! It has no power of its own apart from its Maker. All laws of gravity, all rules of thermodynamics, all calculations of inertia, every human being, and all of creation beyond the earth was and is created and held together by the King of Kings.

Most definitely, this was not the outlandish part of this angel's heavenly heralded news. The outrageous BEHOLDING part, the preposterous part, was that Jesus was the Savior, risen from the tomb of death and destruction. He would take the time, make the time, and share His time to go ahead of the ones who had betrayed Him and given up all hope in Him, and who were part of the humanity that crucified this King of Kings! The angels must have shouted in heaven, "WHAT?" They did not understand GRACE. GRACE was foreign to them. After all, when Satan and one-third of the angels rebelled, there was no looking back; they were banished forever. Jesus did not die for the angels! They can bring the messages, but they cannot understand or relate to the GRACE of THE LORD. Grace is meant only for God's image bearers. This is outstanding, outrageous news; that is why it is called "Good News." The Son of the God of all Creation, who died at humanity's hands, gives unconditional love and mercies to humanity's hearts. This angel of heaven voiced what all angels considered outrageous, "Behold, He is going ahead of you into Galilee; there you will see Him; behold, I have told you."

I would say, "Pay attention, Mary Magdalene and the other Mary; pay attention, disciples; pay attention, us!" He whom you abandoned does not abandon you. You may push Him away, doubt Him, take Him for dead and removed, crucify Him, betray Him, deny Him, or just act like He never existed, but He is going ahead of you. Behold!

Bookends of Beholding Grace!

The bookends of "behold" or the word "indeed" hold up God's glory and grace; Jesus is going ahead of the ones at the grave, and of you and me. What did these unsuspecting partners in resurrection glory do? They set out quickly, interrupted by Hope and Truth; the grave was empty. And of course, these partners took running steps and set out quickly to go tell the men. They didn't hesitate. Would you? Would I? Good question. Let's think about this for today, and BEHOLD, I am not the Savior, and you are not the Savior; Jesus is the Savior.

What do you "behold" or say to yourself, "indeed" about in this story?

Look back at your life and write down the times that Jesus has gone before you.

What can you only dream and hope that Jesus has gone ahead of you for now?

What world events do you want Jesus to go ahead of you for in your life now?

What relationships do you need Jesus to go ahead of you for in your life?

How will you experience Jesus going ahead of you, and how will you trust HIM?

Where else in Scripture does God promise to go before you? (Read John 14.)

Jesus Christ—Son of God over All Creation!

Scene (Seen) 17

Roller Coaster Ride

Matthew 28:9–10

Suddenly Jesus met them and said, "Greetings!" And they came to him, took hold of his feet, and worshiped him. Then Jesus said to them, "Do not be afraid; go and tell my brothers to go to Galilee; there they will see me." (*NRSV*)

Of course, Jesus took baby steps and revealed Himself first to the women, who fell at His feet and worshipped Him; notice their posture for further devotion. Matthew would write in chapter two that the magi saw the Child and fell at His feet and worshipped Him, and this is occurring again now—a fitting response for this Beholding News! Matthew also keeps recording fear throughout these sections: the women were afraid; the guards were afraid; the angel told them not to be afraid; Jesus said not to be afraid. Those putting logical evidence in sequence, in freedom from doubt or fear, would be more believable than the ones that were purely reporting what others witnessed. What I mean is this: for Matthew to write about all the emotions of fear would feed into the truth of this event.

The women left the tomb quickly to tell His disciples. They had come to the tomb somberly and tearfully to serve their dead Jesus. They left the tomb quickly, with fear and great joy. HOW DOES ONE HAVE FEAR AND GREAT JOY at the same time? Fear and great joy when someone you love returns from death? It's possible; think about it. It's the mixture of being on a roller coaster that turns you upside down and seeing that you're in for another twist and flip: fear and great joy.

Roller Coaster Ride

Once, while running up by Colorado Springs, I saw a little ten-year-old boy sitting outside next to a table filled with drawings. They were his artwork; he was selling them. As I ran by, he asked me, "Do you want to buy some artwork?"

I didn't have the heart to say no or run by him without looking. I commented on his passionately penciled and painted drawings, "These are wonderful. Are these all your work?"

He was proud, and responded glowingly, "Yeah, this is my favorite," as he pointed to a drawing of a roller coaster with people riding it. I asked him why it was his favorite, and he responded, "Because my dad and I went on that roller coaster, and one minute my stomach and my eyes were at my feet and the next my feet and stomach were at my eyes. I was so afraid, and laughing at the same time, and it was so cool 'cause my dad was with me!"

So it was with these women who had just left the tomb. Their world had again been turned upside down; their feet ran quickly, and their eyes were beholding. Fear and great joy were not enough for those women; they had divine orders (a divine calling) placed upon them. "Go quickly and tell My brethren…" Whoa! Jesus is calling them by a different name than the angel did; the angel called them "his disciples," but Jesus would call them "My brethren," in forgiveness of betrayal and denial. Jesus calls them HIS BRETHREN. Talk about Grace—there it is, folks. Pay attention, behold, and remember: "My brethren." Not "those guys," not "the sinners," not "the losers," not "the flakes," but "My brethren," spoken by Jesus in forgiveness and mercy. This is the beginning of the Good News, and the women were the bearers of this news. Their lives felt precarious, like my little friend selling his artwork about that roller coaster, and I imagine it was not enough for the Father to watch them experience this. He wanted His Son—the great extension of Himself, Fully Man and Fully God—to be in the middle of this fear and great joy. Jesus came face-to-face with them, and the women fell at His feet like those wise magi from the east in Bethlehem had over thirty years before. The Father was not content to watch from a distance or just send His angelic messengers; He wanted to be with His beloveds. And behold, Jesus met them and greeted them, which was the experience of a lifetime—a roller-coaster ride with Jesus right there. Indeed, He was going before them! He was going before the disciples, but He also had the tenderness to show the women that He was going before them.

They were not forgotten messengers. They were part of His plan, they and the disciples. Jesus wanted to experience that fear and great joy, much as that little boy's father experienced the roller coaster with his son.

How do you experience being invisible in life?

How do you experience roller coasters in life?

Could you believe that Jesus goes before you—that He rides with you?

What would it take to believe this? Why or why wouldn't you?

And for extra reading, read Psalm 139!

By the way, I told the boy, "Sorry, I don't have any money, because I'm just out for a run."

He replied, "That's okay. I think you should have my roller-coaster picture."

I told him, "Oh, no. That's your favorite; I could never take it."

He said, "I want you to have it. I could tell it was your favorite too. And besides, I have another one inside."

I rolled up his picture and ran with it, thanking him with tears in my eyes. I knew it was God's doing. The boy was right and perceptive, as kids so often are. I had been praying earlier that morning, as I started my run—praying for God the Father to show me that He was with me while I was on a life adventure of learning about my own abusive father. I needed to know God the Father.

I wonder if those women at the tomb needed to know their Father God? I believe so. Do you?

Our Father God has the plan; He had it all along. Jesus, Son of Man, Son of God, is the Savior. Confront your fears, and ask Him to show Himself on your roller coaster of life. Then possibly, just possibly, He will reveal His great joys to you a little at a time as you entrust yourself to Him. And remember today: the angel sitting on the rock was right. Behold and behold and behold, Jesus goes before us. Behold!

And by the way, little boy who gave me the roller coaster picture: if you recognize it, I want to pay you for your great advice and your beautiful art work!

Jesus Christ—
Master of Our Roller-coaster Life!

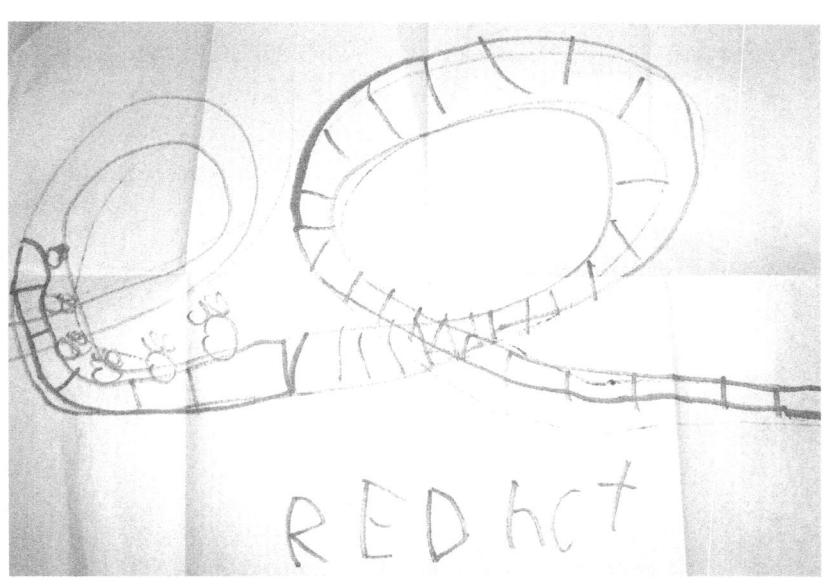

Scene (Seen) 18

Assembling with Elders?

Matthew 28:11–15

While they were going, some of the guards went into the city and told the chief priests everything that had happened. After the priests had assembled with the elders, they devised a plan to give a large sum of money to the soldiers, telling them, "You must say, 'His disciples came by night and stole him away while we were asleep.' If this comes to the governor's ears, we will satisfy him and keep you out of trouble. So they took the money and did as they were directed. And this story is still told among the Jews to this day. (*NRSV*)

What have you and I been "paid off" to do, say, and think, or not to do, not to say, and not to think? "Nothing," we say? Well then—when was the last time we benefitted from putting our desire before another's desire, reputation, power, or popularity?

We all have agendas and plans, and Jesus being alive might just get in the way of our plans and desires. This is how it was while the women were running to tell His brethren on that first day of the week. Those guards were the elite. Their prisoner escaped, and they would have to pay the penalty: death. Their life for their prisoner's life. So, they assembled with the elders. This truly is a sad statement, and one that many of us have experienced, whether inside or outside of those assemblies. If you have been "lucky enough" to be inside the assembly, the question might be: Did you check with the Lord before you voiced your opinion? Or how about the ones who might disagree with you? Did your voice give people a deeper understanding of the reality of the presence of Jesus, or did it speak more about your own presence, position, and platform? Were you just following your own agenda, tagging God's name onto it to make yourself feel good? Did you have peace at the time, and do you have peace now?

These times of unrest, with disease and all of our lack-there-ofs, are a great opportunity for us to get a deeper understanding of so many people who are outside the assembly, rather than the ones "inside" the systems. Most human systems aren't completely right; none have ever been thoroughly right, not even your system, and especially not mine. Eight years ago, thinking I was an insider with influence, I experienced being pushed out of the empowered group. It was a wake-up call for me. Not a wake-up call about who would be hurtful and push me out, but as I stepped into urban ministry, I began the adventure of learning what others experienced from an entirely different perspective. I began realizing the story of my own life of fatherly rejections had made me compassionate to come alongside my brothers and sisters who experienced, on a daily basis, more then I had ever experienced. I had been an insider with an outside history all along.

What do I mean by this? I mean that I didn't know what it was like to have to teach my sons to be careful of what others thought of them, even as they went to the local grocery store. I didn't have to worry about where I was born. I didn't have to worry about food on my table or where it would come from tomorrow. I didn't have to worry about people fearing me because of my skin color. I didn't have to worry about how to figure out a foreign system of living; it was all so familiar, and I was inside.

Who do I have to thank as I look back on these last eight years? I have a friend who comes from the outside and has learned to live for his Lord and his family. I have a family who let me go exploring and encouraged me not to quit. I have friends who prayed. I have a heart that said, "Stay at the table, even when you want to quit," and "Above all else, remember, you are making dinner, helping kids get to camp, paying for their coffees and their lunches, NOT FOR THEM, BUT FOR THE KING." I have the Lord who shows me His ways. He goes before you and I to teach us to be slow to judge, quick to listen and steady to show compassion.

So, my friend, what is your agenda and whom will you serve? Will you stand outside the assemblies of the least? Because the least, according to Jesus, will inherit the kingdom of God. If you haven't had peace, maybe it's time to repent—go to the Lord ALIVE—and say, "I'm so sorry, I've made my life about my agenda. Teach me a new way to live, please." And make that phone call or face-to-face meeting to own your part of the "assembled together" moment and to ask for forgiveness. It's never too late!

The saddest part of this story in Scripture was that these were "elders," the wise ones! So—age doesn't make one wise. They gave money to the soldiers, promised to talk to the politician, and made a smooth path for these elite soldiers. We all must learn to be wiser about the promises we make, the assembling we do, our agendas, and our views. No matter how hard we try, Scripture clearly tells us, in Romans 3:23, "For all have sinned and fallen short of the glory of God."

Now, if you are the one outside the assembly, outside the ones who lied and paid off others, don't be too quick in your relief. We all must be cautious in how we speak of others, even the ones who have hurt us—especially them. Notice Matthew's words, perhaps of warning: "And this story was widely spread among the Jews, and is to this day." The Jews, not the Romans—the ones in the assembly, oppressing, were telling this story! How did they tell it? Whose side were they on? (That's always the question, it seems.) I wonder which parts were false news, or just more agendas floating around? What stories do you and I spread, even to this day? Do we spread stories of truth and grace and mercy, or just "our" stories?

Assembling with Elders?

Some thought Jesus was dead, His body stolen. Some knew not what happened but spread the story to this day. What stories are you and I spreading? No, there is no one who does good all the time and everywhere, no one! So—what do we do?

Start with Jesus Alive. He knows the stories circulating. He knows the agendas. Trust Him to be your shield, which may mean speaking up and having a voice, but just remember that He says to go to the source, not to others. Trust Him to be your shield, and that probably means not getting revenge, but trust in Him. He knows those soldiers; He knows the elders; He knows the disciples hiding; He knows the women; He knows the liars and those who seem to be in control; He knows even the injustices, and always the truths. Jesus goes before all of this; go to Jesus and read His words of mercy, His words of turning tables over, His words of love and words of warning.

> What might this Scripture be bringing up in your life—maybe injustices you have done, or that have been done to you? Time to learn to heal. No lie could hold Him to the tomb. No grave could keep Him captive.

> Bring your injustices to Jesus, in prayer to the risen King—bring the one who cast you out, or who you cast out, and see that Jesus has risen and is victorious. Then, in the words of His mother, Mary, on that first day of miracles at a wedding feast (John 2:5), "Whatever he says to you, do it." Do it because Jesus lives. How could we not follow Him? How could you or I NOT obey Him?

Jesus Christ—Shield to All Who Come to Him!

Scene (Seen) 19

A Mountainous Moment

Matthew 28:16–17

Now the eleven disciples went to Galilee, to the mountain to which Jesus had directed them. When they saw him, they worshiped him; but some doubted. (*NRSV*)

The eleven walked and walked. They walked from Jerusalem to Galilee, a designated mountain—seventy miles! What did they think about on their journey? Did they pass by memorable spots where Jesus healed, Jesus taught, Jesus hugged, and Jesus laughed and wept? Were they silent, or were they talking about the next sporting event or political move? I imagine that Peter chattered, John was pensive, Andrew ran ahead of Peter, and Nathaniel and Thomas questioned. Were James and the rest praying and talking about the next place they would eat?

And the women, what happened to them? Well, I think they followed or maybe ran ahead of these newborn leaders. They walked as a church; they walked forward, and they walked in fear and faith, belief and doubt. They walked and processed and walked some more. I am pretty sure there were moments when they didn't want to walk anymore; seventy miles is a lot of walking. Did their human logic pull at their feet with the question, "How could Jesus be alive?" Did their cynical nature rear its head and speak words like, "This is a waste of time, a chasing after wind?"

A Mountainous Moment

Did the doubts hover over them like thick clouds in a wilderness? (How very similar to their ancestors wandering in the wilderness.) Or did they talk about the wonder of Jesus resurrected? What would all of this mean for them personally? Did they recite the prophet Isaiah's words as they walked through the day and night?

Isaiah 40:28–31

Have you not known? Have you not heard? The LORD is the everlasting God, the Creator of the ends of the earth. He does not faint or grow weary; his understanding is unsearchable. He gives power to the faint and strengthens the powerless. Even youths will faint and be weary, and the young will fall exhausted, but those who wait for the LORD shall renew their strength; they shall mount up with wings like eagles; they shall run and not be weary; they shall walk and not faint. *(NRSV)*

Did the young and humorous Mark, the one mentored by Peter, who would later write the first Gospel, make them laugh as they walked and talked? After all, he could have been recounting the moment when the soldiers were arresting Jesus, and Mark came, wearing just a linen sheet, and tried to stop them. "They grabbed him. But he pulled free of the linen sheet and escaped naked" (Mark 14:51–52).

Did they know everything at that point, in the middle of their walk? Jesus had shown up to them a few times before; that will be discussed in the other Gospel accounts. Trudging over mountainous desert trails for seventy miles would make any traveler mature in their thinking and life wisdom. Did they all reflect, at some point, about that time with Jesus when chaos and confusion came into the peaceful Gethsemane garden, and their King of Kings was arrested, and they ran away, abandoning Him? **Can you relate?**

When you're asked to "go the extra mile" and you have nothing left to give—not one more step you're able take (that's why they call it the "extra mile")—you have a choice to make: take the extra mile or quit. The moment of light is right around the next corner; DON'T QUIT.

And then their walk was finished—just when they couldn't walk another step; it was over. "When they saw Him, they worshipped Him; but some were doubtful" (Matt. 28:17). They saw Him and worshipped Him—what must that reunion have looked like? A mountainous moment, one of great joy and fear, hope and doubt, with an outward focus on Jesus and an inward introspection; their thoughts were on their faith, both past and present. They worshipped, and still some were doubtful, now utterly convinced they could not fix anything, for they were NOT the Savior.

What will it take for each of us to follow and walk the extra mile, worship, and NOT doubt?

Let's not fool ourselves or cast lofty judgment on these seventy-mile-struggling seekers of Jesus! We might worship on a Sunday, but sometime in the next week we will doubt, if only for a flashing moment. It's okay, Jesus expects it. He doesn't turn the seekers away. Instead, Jesus challenges them with four commands. Those commands are each meant for a different devotion, a different day, a different deliberation in their questioning minds and hearts—and of course, ours too; let's be honest! But for today, we are faced with the challenge:

How far will you follow Jesus, worshipping? How will you risk being real to the risen Jesus, knowing that He understands your fears, your joys, and your doubts?

FOR NOW, JUST REST AND REFLECT AND PRAY
FOR STRENGTH FOR THE JOURNEY.

Jesus Christ—the Author and Completion!

Scene (Seen) 20

Breathe Easy, All Authority Is Jesus

Matthew 28:18-20

And Jesus came and said to them, "All authority in heaven and on earth has been given to me. Go therefore and make disciples of all nations, baptizing them in the name of the Father and of the Son and of the Holy Spirit, and teaching them to obey everything that I have commanded you. And remember, I am with you always, to the end of the age." (*NRSV*)

*A*nd "Jesus came up..." Was he walking up to them? In that culture, it was proper and good for the disciple, the one being mentored, to come up to the rabbi as a sign of respect. Jesus comes up to them! Look back at when Jesus appeared to the women. They knew their position: "And they came up and took hold of his feet and worshiped Him" (Matt. 28:9). Their position was one in which Jesus was the respected teacher, rabbi, and Lord, so their position was at his feet. Jesus comes up to His brethren: the seventy-mile stragglers, the questioning, the meek, the poor, the weak and the strong, and the exhausted. Again, Jesus initiates the relationship. NOTICE THIS. Jesus always starts the relationship. He always does the initiating work of pursuing doubtful hearts. When one reads, "And Jesus came up," one should pause in wonder and respect. All the angels behold this as marvelous. **Why don't we who follow Christ remember this?**

"All authority has been given Me in heaven and on earth" (Matt. 28: 19). Not some, but **all** authority. He has been given all *exousia* which means, "permission, power of authority, choosing all freedom of power (physically and mentally)" (Strongs, 1849). Jesus has been given all the influential power and privileges due to the King of Kings.

I find it interesting that Jesus didn't need to speak about His authority with the women; they were familiar with a lower position. But His disciples might have needed to be reminded. He doesn't tell them, "Don't be afraid." Instead, he goes straight to his authority. Maybe it was because he knew the trials they would face, and Jesus knew this would be an encouraging and important part of what they needed to really get into their hearts and minds. Understanding that he is in charge, Jesus encourages his disciples to keep doing what they were doing. "Go."

The word "Go" is not a command from Jesus to His disciples. It is an *aorist* passive verb, which means a continuous form of a verb; it's always happening—past, present, and future. They were always going, always continuing on journey, like us. Go. The disciples go to the market, go to the synagogue, go to the meeting places, go to the seas, go to the courts, go to the everyday places. They will go home, go to sleep, go to their families and friends, and go the distance. Jesus reminds them that he has full authority. They are under his domain, and they have gone, will go, and will be going. Oh, the glorious kingdom of heaven on earth! We have gone, are going, and will be going under all the authority of Jesus, given to him by God the FATHER—the God we are privileged to call "Our Father, who art in the skies" (Bruner). We are not the Savior; all authority is Jesus' authority, and his alone.

How has Jesus initiated a relationship with you?

What authority of His might you be usurping or not valuing?

How have you been "Going" these days?

How are you "Going" now?

How will you "Go?" And what will you understand that brings hope to you?

Jesus Christ—GOD to Whom All Authority Belongs!

Scene (Seen) 21

BEHOLD HIM!

Matthew 28:18–20

And Jesus came and said to them, "All authority in heaven and on earth has been given to me. Go therefore and make disciples of all nations, baptizing them in the name of the Father and of the Son and of the Holy Spirit, and teaching them to obey everything that I have commanded you. And remember, I am with you always, to the end of the age." (*NRSV*)

The "therefore" is there for a reason! Because Jesus Christ has all authority in heaven and on earth, all who are created by Him for the purpose of carrying out the image of the Father, Son, and Holy Spirit are commanded by Jesus to go and to do amazing service. This is not just for the elite eleven. These are commands for all. After all, it will take everyone to complete this audacious task! So then, I ask you and myself, what is God's part, and what is His followers' part? Take time to read the Scripture and list out the responsibilities:

GOD'S PART	MY/YOUR PART

Which one do you want to try to obey?

Wait a minute; do we have a choice?

Jesus is talking to His beloveds. According to Matthew, Jesus spoke to them all with one breath, issuing four commands for all His followers:

1. "Make disciples" meant to teach and instruct followers of Jesus. The Greek word is *Matheteuo* which means to enroll as a scholar (Strongs, G3100). They were to train up from all the nations, not just some.

2. "Baptizing them in the name of the Father, Son, and Holy Spirit." Baptism requires two: the one baptizing and the one being baptized. But the claim over the one being baptized is a three-named claim: the Father, the Son, and the Holy Spirit. Jesus' followers are to baptize all the nations—to "make" disciples of them, claiming them in the names of THE ONES who created those nations and their peoples. Those who are baptized are given the Father, the Son, and the Holy Spirit; what more could one want?

3. "Teaching them to observe all that I commanded you." Well, that will take a lifetime of discipling, not just a short time on a street corner making quick converts, a one-week camp experience, or a one-time call in front of the church. Teaching them to observe all Jesus' commands could take at least three years of discipleship. After all, the disciples spent three years following Jesus, and the rest of their lifetime following the Holy Spirit, all in the name of the Father, Son, and the Holy Spirit.

There are three easily found commands; remember, "Go" is a continuous verb, not a command. Jesus knows that the disciples will continually be on the go! So, where is the fourth command? Well, it might be easier to notice if we study "God's Part":

1. Verse 18 states that all authority has been given to Him in heaven and on earth. It is Jesus' responsibility to create earth as it is in heaven. It is God's part.

2. Verse 19 states that Jesus has given the disciples all of His commands—not some, but all.

3. "I am with you always, even to the end of the age." Jesus promises to be with the disciples to the end of the age. This phrase is the word *aion*, which means: "forever, an unbroken age, perpetually in time, and eternity; the worlds, universe; period of time, age" (Strong, 165). Did Jesus promise to be with only His disciples until their end? No, Jesus promises to eternally be with you, me, the disciples, and those who follow His future, forever—unbroken age!

So, where is the fourth command? The fourth command has been omitted or tucked away in the simple word "lo" in others. "Lo" is an elderly word; in the ancient Greek language, it is the word *idou*. *This word was, seemingly, one of* Matthew's favorite words, meaning "behold, see, perceive, pay attention." This word, *idou*, would appear fifty-nine times in the twenty-eight chapters of Matthew. Matthew, the tax collector, had a lifetime of beholding Jesus, and I believe the reason he uses this word over forty times in his Gospel is that he had spent the first part of his life missing the Father God, cheating others, and refusing to recognize those he was cheating as the ones whom God had wonderfully created. Maybe as Matthew was writing this, he didn't want to miss God the Father anymore! He didn't want anyone who read this Gospel to miss God either. God didn't want anyone to miss this most important command: beholding Jesus eternally. Jesus doesn't want you, me, the ancient readers of this text, or Matthew, the writer of this text, to be so consumed with the commands of God, to "make disciples, baptize disciples, teach disciples," that we all would miss the whole point of the story. The point of this writing was and is: Jesus is with Matthew, the disciples, you, me, and future followers for all eternity.

This was what the angel wanted to make sure the women at the tomb knew: "Behold, He is going ahead of you into Galilee; there you will see Him. Behold, I have told you." Jesus is past, present, and future. The angel who announced this to the woman at the tomb, bookended by the statement, "Behold," wants everyone to know. Why in the world have some chosen to omit one of the greatest commands we, as believers in Christ, have been given?

Follower of Jesus, never—for all eternity—never forget to "Behold." Remember it always!

"Behold, I am with you eternally, wherever you are" (Matt. 28:20).

How will you see Jesus today?

How might you have missed Jesus yesterday?

What will you do to behold Jesus for eternity?

Now, continue and GO.

What is your example of Beholding?

I like to watch a fountain pad where small fountains go up and down, with water splashing and children dancing. They are called splash pads. A mother puts down her baby, who can crawl in the middle of this splash pad, where fountains rise up and down—a pure delight for this little one. Some children stand in the middle of the fountain, risking the rising waters and celebrating their wonder. Other children slowly walk up and down these cascades of crystal liquid and celebrate the sound but not the touch. Others hold hands at the edge, risking their toes to feel the pulse of these seemingly alive waters. Others wait for their parents to hold them tight in these loud, rushing pools of joy. Some children dance around these waters as if the fountains were their dance partners. However, they experience the fountains, one thing is certain: the fountains exist, and they are a wonder, a delight, and a curiosity to all. They behold all, in some manner or another.

One sure thing, according to the Gospel writer Matthew: Jesus Christ is real, and a pure delight of eternity to behold. Let us behold Jesus as these little ones behold the waters, or as the women at the tomb, the wise Magi, or the eleven disciples beheld. Behold Jesus, worship at His feet, come questioning, but don't stop coming to splash in the waters of His cleansing Love and Grace and Mercies. They are refreshing and eternal, and He will never leave you or forsake you.

Jesus Christ—GOD to Behold!

Scene (Seen) 22

Cookies or Dirt?

Luke 23:50–56

Now there was a good and righteous man named Joseph, who, though a member of the council, had not agreed to their plan and action. He came from the Jewish town of Arimathea, and he was waiting expectantly for the kingdom of God. This man went to Pilate and asked for the body of Jesus. Then he took it down, wrapped it in a linen cloth, and laid it in a rock-hewn tomb where no one had ever been laid. It was the day of Preparation, and the sabbath was beginning. The women who had come with him from Galilee followed, and they saw the tomb and how his body was laid. Then they returned, and prepared spices and ointments. On the sabbath they rested according to the commandment. (*NRSV*)

*W*ho is Luke? He was a doctor.

We have a friend who is a doctor. He is a neurosurgeon, a brain surgeon—the really smart kind. I met him while he was doing his residency; he is of Jewish descent, and he loves the Lord Jesus Christ and calls Him the Messiah. Dave wanted to serve the Lord in some capacity, wanted to be hands-on with people and learn to share his faith. He would come over all the time for dinner with our family, and he was shocked at all of the happenings in a house full of boys and kids from Young Life—never a dull moment. He was and is brilliant, and the depth of his heritage was refreshing. I love to hear about others' stories, their cultures, traditions, thoughts, and lifestyles. We became great friends, and at one point he decided he would love to be able to hang out with teenagers and serve the Lord in leadership. He quickly became a leader, and finally, one evening at the gathering, he was talked into being in a humorous skit.

We were doing a spoof on the old children's morning television show, *Mister Rogers' Neighborhood..* In the skit, Mister Rogers was planting plants and talking to his friend about the four food groups. Dave was playing the part of Mister Rogers. He was perfect for it, a neat and particular kind of guy who was extreme about his diet for that time (twenty-five years ago). The goal of the skit was to talk about the food groups with Mister Rogers's friend, Mr. McFeely, and then show him different food groups and do a taste test. When he got to the bread group, he would have no bread to taste, so he would say, "Mr. McFeely, did you know bread comes from the ground? And did you know that a seed is planted in the ground? That I have earth in this pot, and then it rises up to become wheat, and then the wheat becomes bread?"

Mr. McFeely would say, "No Mister Rogers, I didn't know that."

And then Mister Rogers would say, "Yep. And since we don't have any bread to taste, I bet we could eat this dirt that the seeds were planted into as an example of our fourth food group."

Obviously, the crowd of teenagers would break out with, "Eat it, eat it, eat it." And before Mr. McFeely could stop him, he would put a large handful of dirt in his mouth. What the kids in the audience didn't know was that the dirt in the pot was really Oreo cookies ground up so they looked like dirt, though obviously they weren't. So, the kids would be yelling and laughing as Mister Rogers put a large helping of dirt into his mouth and chewed it up. The lights would go out, and the skit would end. I love Young Life laughter and skits; the sarcasm and ridiculous one-line jokes make everyone laugh. Laughter is good and, in our world, we need a lot of it. It actually breaks down walls of people and it seems to bring a healing.

Dave trusted me to grind up the cookies and prepare the "dirt" in the pot for him. But what he didn't know was that I was in a prankish mood, and *I decided to put real dirt in the pot.* When he

Cookies or Dirt?

raised the dirt to his mouth in the skit, he could smell that it was real dirt and had to decide what to do. All of the other leaders knew his plight, and we were all in the back of the room, laughing and watching as he bravely placed the dirt in his mouth. He had a mouthful of dirt, and the lights stayed up long enough for his eyes to get really big, with laughter bellowing from the high school friends and me beginning to feel guilty. Dave would never do that skit again; I can't understand why not! What's amazing was that I could get it past him and onto the table, because he is a man of drastic detail. There's more to say about this story, but suffice it to say that he has a good-natured heart, is a man of deep joy, and is still our good friend to this day, despite my antics.

Dr. Luke was just such a man: an intelligent, schooled learner, a physician who researched, questioned, and listened to the ones who had followed Jesus. Like Dave, he was scrupulous about details, examining everything said to him about this Son of Man, whom Luke called "Lord Jesus." He would be one of the adventuring doctors, writing in a very academic Greek to tell the story of Jesus in his Gospel, as well as the story of the early followers of Jesus after His ascension into heaven, written in the book called Acts. Luke would attend Paul on many of his journeys. I'm sure he was a great encourager to Paul. Luke would write with the visual—the story of Jesus' dead body, Joseph of Arimathea, and the others involved—with precision, pointing at highlights that he, Dr. Luke, thought to be crucial. We learn more about Joseph as a member of the council, a good and righteous man who did not consent to the council's plans to kill Jesus, a man of Arimathea who was waiting for the kingdom of God. He described Joseph as a man of action who went to Pilate and asked for Jesus' body, then laid it in a tomb cut into the rock, where no one had ever before been placed.

Why are these details so important?

Details bring validity to a story and reveal its truths. Notice that Luke shares how the women watched where Joseph would place the body so they could leave to prepare. What did they prepare? They prepared spices and perfume. And then they rested, in obedience to the commandment to keep the Sabbath holy and reserved for rest.

Luke was not Jewish; he was Greek. Yet Luke was aware of culture, paid attention to detail, and was an observer of many types of people, always watching and always listening. Why is this important? Coming from a skeptical mentality myself, these Scriptures were very impactful because in them I saw how there were so many different kinds of men who wrote about Jesus: Dr. Luke; Matthew, a tax collector; Mark a young apprentice of Peter; and John, the older soul. As you read Luke's version of the resurrection, may you be keenly aware of the fine details, and may you take great hope from the fact that the scientific side of mankind was well represented by Dr. Luke.

> **What questions might you and I ask, this time around, in the reading of the records of Jesus alive?**

> I would suggest paying attention to details and asking:

> **Why would Dr. Luke be writing this?**

> **Why is this story, rather than another story, so significant to Dr. Luke?**

> **Why is this important to me, personally, now?**

Details are critical. Details illustrate the truth of the story. Unlike me, Dr. Luke was not deceiving. Dr. Luke had an impeccable integrity to get to the bottom of the story and reveal its truth. His words would ring true:

> Inasmuch as many have undertaken to compile an account of the things accomplished among us, just as they were handed down to us by those who from the beginning were eyewitnesses and servants of the word, it seemed fitting for me as well, having investigated everything carefully from the beginning, to write it out for you in consecutive order" (Luke 1:1–3).

Oh, and by the way, Dave, you have my public apology about the dirt. And thanks for being a faithful doctor and friend, like Dr. Luke.

Today, look for details of your own life in your reading of Luke, and try to find God's hand in the midst of these details.

Jesus Christ— the God of All Details!

Scene (Seen) 23

The LIVING ONE

*D*r. Luke would describe Jesus the Nazarene as the Christ, the Sacrificing Servant, and the Lord Jesus. He ends chapter twenty-three just as a doctor would declare someone dead: somber in spirit, merciful to the loved ones of the deceased, but factual—Jesus was dead. This would be critical in the mind of the scientist, Dr. Luke, and over and over again, this would be his description of the Risen Jesus as well. Jesus was "delivered into the hands of sinful men, crucified to death." If left with this news in Luke 23, one would say, "Well, that's a tragic story." BUT! The good doctor would begin the next part of his graphic story with the word "But," as if HOPE had exploded in the midst of GRAVE NEWS. And it did!

> *Luke 24:1–5*
>
> But on the first day of the week, at early dawn, they came to the tomb bringing the spices which they had prepared. ² And they found the stone rolled away from the tomb, ³ but when they entered, they did not find the body of the Lord Jesus. ⁴ While they were perplexed about this, behold, two men suddenly stood near them in dazzling clothing; ⁵ and as *the women* were terrified and bowed their faces to the ground, *the men* said to them, "Why do you seek the living One among the dead?" (*NRSV*)

Notice the words he uses to describe the women, reporting the time and date: early dawn on the first day of the week. Morning comes for the followers of Jesus. They came, Luke writes, with the dead Jesus in mind, bringing the spices they had prepared for this dead Jesus.

My question is this: If the believers wanted to convince others that Jesus was alive, why would they write about their short-sighted vision and boast of it?

The fact was that they were going to anoint the dead body of Jesus. That would put doubt in the mind of anyone who read these facts. They found the stone rolled away, and Luke would then record the astounding words, beginning with "But" again. It was almost as if Luke saw the facts and was astounded, as he would write the next word: "But when they entered, they did not find the body of the Lord Jesus." Notice that Dr. Luke does not jump to conclusions, BUT does list the facts:

- Early dawn
- First day of the week
- Bringing spices to anoint dead Jesus
- Stone rolled away
- No human body in the tomb
- Women perplexed, meaning "in doubt, not to know which way to turn, to be at a loss with one's self" (Strong, G639)

The women were at a loss. For at this great moment, they saw their works were not needed, not necessary—futile, and a loss.

What might they have been feeling or thinking? What would you feel and think? Have you ever been in a place in life where none of your efforts work and you have nothing left to bring to the table, and it seems like no one needs you or wants you?

One friend—more like a son to us than just our four sons' friend—was diagnosed with cancer. Nothing could be done; all answers had been extinguished. I would be planning my day and he would call me from his hospital room. "Hey, Mase, let's talk. Can you bring me a vanilla shake?"

I would always say yes to that question. There was nothing left for me to do but buy a vanilla shake and go spend time with our Troy. This time, he wanted to tell me a story. He wanted to tell me the story of when he coded during a cancer treatment. It was not the story of what the doctors and nurses did; it was the story of what he experienced when they could do nothing as he lay on the hospital bed.

I came in with his vanilla shake, and he told me, "Mase, I will never make fun of you again for being emotional when you talk about Jesus. Mase, never!"

I told him, "Troy, I love it when you make fun of me; it keeps me light about myself and serious about Christ." He then proceeded to give me a description that only he and I could share about Jesus and His compassion.

After Troy described this experience to me (one of seeing Jesus in bright light and knowing that Jesus knew him and was inviting him), as my eyes fought back tears, he said, "Mase, you don't have to worry about me. I'm going to be all right. I saw Jesus—real, live Jesus. Really, Mase. I will be all right." I believed him.

That is exactly what Dr. Luke wants to explain. The women saw these men as dazzling white, as Dr. Luke described them. Matthew and John called them angels, but Dr. Luke might have had a hard time writing that into his manuscript, being a physician and an academic. Nevertheless, Dr. Luke proceeds to report that the women would fall on their faces terrified, bowing their faces to the ground. No one bows for any man as a Jew! They bowed, but that was not Dr. Luke's main emphasis! What were these men who were in dazzling clothing? The word "dazzling" is "*astrapto*," which means, "to lighten" (Strong, 797). These men in dazzling clothing seemed to be astounded that the women would ever believe Jesus would stay dead. Why in the world would the women ever consider that a crucifixion would stop Jesus, or that a stone would stop Jesus, or that guards and a government would stop Jesus, or DEATH itself?

So the men ask the monumental question that Dr. Luke proclaims, which should be written in broad, dramatically italicized strokes:

"Why do you seek the Living One among the dead?"

It was the same theme that Troy would speak to me about that day in the hospital. "Don't worry about me, Kathy; it was beautiful. I saw Him. Don't worry about me. Kathy, Jesus is real and alive. Don't worry about me."

I don't blame those women at that tomb—I would have been shocked as well—because of what I seek in my own life. I seek **power, popularity,** and **possessions** to satisfy me. Yes, these are the dead things I seek. Might all of us do this? And guess what? It started with Genesis 3:6:

> When the woman saw that the tree was good for food, and that it was a delight to the eyes, and that the tree was desirable to make *one* wise, she took from its fruit and ate; and she gave also to her husband with her, and he ate.

The woman and her husband saw that something other than God could be good for food—possessions can fill us. The woman and her husband saw that the tree (the idol, other than God Himself) was a delight to the eyes, that would be filling the pleasing nature that they needed to be filled to be a delight in each other's eyes. The woman and her husband saw that the tree (the idol, other than God Himself) was desirable to make one wise—to have power or be in control.

> **How do you and I seek power? Do we seek it by putting down others who are different, or who disagree with us? Do we shame each other on social media?**
>
> **How do I seek popularity? What's the first thing you and I look at on our social media feeds—how many "likes" we have?**
>
> **Or how about not wanting to stick up for the marginalized out of fear of what your friends might think?**

How do I seek possessions? Do I make it my goal in life to strive for comforts? What do we seek?

Here are the three temptations known to all humanity. They embellish themselves as being able to carry the weight of what we live for, but in no way are they meant to be our gods. They fail. They were not created to carry the weight! These are the temptations known to us all, but the attack isn't centered on us, as if we were the center of history and life. The attack is on the Living God, for if we choose to strive after possessions, popularity, or power, we are saying, "GOD IS NOT ENOUGH." Ultimately, the attack is against the God of all creation.

What is astounding is that as followers of God, we have popularity—the God of all has His eyes on us. We have power—the God of all justice has called us to be His image bearers, with power and rule as He gives it. And we have possessions—the God of Creation's full desire is for us to rule, subduing all through Him, who is ENOUGH. The reason I know this, and Dr. Luke knows this, and the women know this, is that Jesus is the LIVING ONE; all else is dead in comparison.

So why is it that we seek the Living One among the dead, or that which is a fake for possessional fulfillment, popularity fulfillment, and power fulfillment?

Great question! Maybe you and I need to think through the reasons—the whys—of what we believe about the LIVING ONE.

Troy told me, "Kathy, I'm going to be fine. Love you, Kath."

The reason Troy could say this is that he saw the LIVING ONE, he had surrendered his life and will to Jesus, and he had entrusted himself, and his loved ones, to Jesus Christ the Living One. He knew Jesus was enough.

How does this look for you? Is the dead:
- Obsession with something comfortable, materialism—possessions?

The LIVING ONE

- Obsession with a relationship—popularity?
- Obsession with a title, control—power?

Living life is more than just obtaining these. Oh, that we would be obsessed with the LIVING ONE! What would it look like if, in my life or yours, the emphasis was on the LIVING ONE?

What if it meant bringing spices—our works—to the feet of Jesus, and then, breathing in His love, laying them there, not in striving but in peace?

What does peace look like for you as you expect the LIVING ONE in your living life?

Jesus Christ—the Living One!

Scene (Seen) 24

Not a Moment to Lose!

Luke 24:6–9

He is not here, but He has risen. Remember how He spoke to you while He was still in Galilee, ⁷ saying that the Son of Man "must be delivered into the hands of sinful men, and be crucified, and the third day rise again." And they remembered His words, ⁹ and returned from the tomb and reported all these things to the eleven and to all the rest. (NRSV)

The Living One reveals Himself in the stories that Dr. Luke writes, and all those who read are challenged to remember. Before we get started this time, write down all that you need to remember today.

List:

The angelic men tell the women, "He is not here; He is risen." The emphasis of the angelic men was not on themselves but centered all their focus on Christ. From the angelic men, the essence of what mattered was the following:

1. "Jesus spoke to you."
2. The specific time when Jesus was speaking to them, which the angels wanted them to remember: "while He was still in Galilee."
3. As recorded in Luke, the last time Jesus was in Galilee, He was teaching His disciples and friends and foretold His second coming (Luke 17). Jesus called Himself "Son of Man" at this time.
4. Jesus was recorded by Luke as saying, "But first He must suffer many things and be rejected by this generation" (Luke 17:25).
5. The "men"—angels—reminded the women that Jesus said, "He must be delivered into the hands of sinful men" (Luke 24:7).
6. The "men" reminded these women that Jesus said, "I must be crucified" (Luke 24:7).
7. The "men" reminded the women that Jesus said, "On the third day, I will rise again" (Luke 24:7).

The angels told the women what Jesus told them in Galilee. There were many times when Jesus was in Galilee; maybe the angels were referring to the moment recorded in Luke 9:22, after He fed the crowds of over five thousand people. Remember when He asked the disciples, "But who do you say that I am?" And Peter answered, "the Christ of God" (Luke 9:20). They were remembering the joy of being fed, being loved by the crowds, and thinking things were going well for all who followed Jesus.

Peter would answer Jesus, "the Christ of God," meaning the anointed of God. But Jesus would warn them that it wasn't going to go the way they thought. He warned them and instructed *them* not to tell this to anyone, saying, "The Son of Man must suffer many things and be rejected by the elders and chief priests and scribes, and be killed and be raised up on the third day."

And He was saying to *them* all, "If anyone wishes to come after Me, he must deny himself, and take up his cross daily and follow Me'" (Luke 9:21–23).

The angels reminded the women that if anyone wanted to follow Jesus, they had to deny themselves, take up their cross, and follow Jesus. What does "deny self" look like from the perspective of possessions, popularity, and power? Luke recorded that after the angel men had spoken, the women remembered, returned from the place of death, and reported all to the eleven friends of Jesus. The women:

REMEMBERED
RETURNED
REPORTED

Three great action words that Luke wrote about the women, and these words are powerful because the women accomplished much. They remembered Jesus' words prior to his death while he was in Galilee, they returned from the dead places of life, and then they reported to the eleven, and to all the rest who were in Jerusalem. The words they might have remembered would have been the words that Jesus spoke about his being raised from the dead. May I suggest the dead places of life are those places where possessions, popularity, and power are the priorities of life—the constant focus of their lives, as well as our lives?

Who were these women, according to Dr. Luke? They were Mary Magdalene, Joanna, Mary, who was the mother of James, and the other women with them. We know about the two women named Mary, as recorded by Matthew, but who is Joanna? Joanna was the wife of Chuza, King Herod's steward. Joanna's husband held a significant position as the guardian of Herod's household. He carried great power as he would manage the properties of Herod. Remember that Herod was the one Pilate sent Jesus to during the trial of Jesus. Herod and Pilate would become friends after that time. Chuza carried an official title, one of prestige and power. What would the official's wife be doing hanging around with the followers of Jesus, let alone showing up at the grave of this so-called criminal, Jesus? Mary Magdalene, Joanna's friend, who had been healed of being possessed by seven demons, was right alongside these women. Joanna knew Jesus was worth more than any possession she or her husband owned, more than any popularity the courts of King Herod could entertain, more than the power of any official title. Jesus was the Messiah. She knew this because He had healed her, as recorded in Luke 8:2–3: "And *also* some women who had been healed of evil spirits and sicknesses: Mary who was called Magdalene, from whom seven demons had gone out, ³ and Joanna the wife of Chuza, Herod's steward, and Susanna, and many others who were contributing to their support out of their private means." Joanna knew who Jesus was—GOD. Later, Joanna would courageously use her resources for the benefit of the church because she knew Jesus was the One who heals and alive.

All these women did the obvious thing after bringing spices to anoint a dead body and finding out that Jesus was alive: they remembered what Jesus had said when He was in Galilee, returned from the empty tomb of Jesus, and reported what they had heard about Jesus!

> Today, what will you remember that Jesus has done for you in your past?
>
> Today, how will you return in your own life and see Jesus as the Living One?
>
> Today, what will you report about Jesus?
>
> What are you waiting for? There's not a moment to lose!

Jesus Christ—the Christ of God!

Scene (Seen) 25

What If?

Luke 24:10–12

Now they were Mary Magdalene and Joanna and Mary the mother of James; also the other women with them were telling these things to the apostles. But these words appeared to them as nonsense, and they would not believe them. But Peter got up and ran to the tomb; stooping and looking in, he saw the linen wrappings only; and he went away to his home, marveling at what had happened. (*NRSV*)

How quick are you and I to listen to each other, or to others in our lives? How quick are you and I to communicate back what we have heard in the form of questions—listening to the details, taking interest, slowing down, not making judgments? In the world of crisis management, COVID, or the crisis of racial injustice, it is essential to "slow down."

I was at a Young Life camp, heading into a staff meeting—there's always a meeting to go to, isn't there! A leader was sitting on a bench, taking a breather from being with her twelve high school friends. As I walked behind the bench, hurrying to the meeting, I sensed that maybe the Lord wanted me to slow down and ask her what was going on.

I knew I would be late to the meeting if I stopped, but I had read Psalm 42 that morning: "As the deer pants for the water brooks, so my soul pants for You, O God. My soul thirsts for God, for the living God; When shall I come and appear before God?"

I remembered that the Lord reminds me to slow down and

What If?

thirst for the Lord, not to please others by being on time for a meeting but to please God. This leader was in a moment that no one would know except the Lord, who knew, and He had been preparing my heart to stop, seek out, and be present.

How little I knew, though, for God's ways are higher than our ways, always! So—sensing a nudge but not recognizing it was the Lord, like a little kid wearing their daddy's large shoes and clomping around, I stopped and asked, "Hey, how are you this morning?"

She answered, "Okay. My husband is in the military and has been gone for combat drills, so I haven't seen him in two months. When he was able to come home, I had committed to my YL girls to go to camp, so he is home right now and I am here. Then, when I go home, he will be gone for another couple of months." She said this with tears in her eyes, trying to be brave.

I stopped in my tracks. Stopping in the middle of busyness is essential—stopping, asking questions, and then listening. I said, "Wait, so you are telling me that you sacrificed seeing your husband so you could be with your YL kids at camp and share the Gospel? Wow!" Then I asked her, "How long before you will see him again?"

She replied, "I don't know, maybe a few more months."

Then I said, "So he's home now for a week, but you are here?" Her reply, with tears in her eyes but courage in her voice, was, "Yes. But we both know I need to be here to share about the love of Jesus and how He is alive and lives in us." Her faith was astounding!

I asked her if I could pray for her. I told her it was a privilege to meet her and that I would like to spend more time with her in the afternoon. We became friends instantly. She was volunteering, and I loved her heart for the Lord and her high school friends. She was giving all she had for the opportunity to tell her friends about the God of hope, about the Cross story of Christ and the miraculous resurrection, meaning that He is alive and will one day restore all life. He will restore the times sacrificed for our loved ones; He will restore the broken. He will restore the captives, as is written by the songwriter in Psalms: "Oh, that the salvation of Israel would come out of Zion! When God restores His captive people, Let Jacob rejoice, let Israel be glad" (Psalm 53:6).

Not only did the alive Jesus bring a restorative message of hope for His early followers, but He gives us great joy and hope for the present as well. I mean, what if tomorrow He restored our health, our love of others, our future? He will, because He is alive, and this is what the early followers were discovering. Jesus was alive, and this meant He conquered death, and those who follow Him will be alive one day!

In the Scripture written by Luke, the women came to tell the disciples, and they didn't believe the women! Yes, this is grievous, but God is bigger than this! Luke will record that Peter ran to the tomb to peek; thank God for Peter. The Gospel writer, John, will write about it and share that it was both he and Peter who would go to that tomb. Why? Did Peter and John have an idea that maybe, just maybe, Jesus was alive?

What would change for you if Jesus was alive?

What hope would you have?

What would this mean for you?

What hope would the resurrection of Jesus have for the leader that I just described? What hope could I give her that day?

Well, I shared this with my team at camp, and so we prayed. As we prayed, I got an idea. I went to the camp manager after the meeting and told him my idea. What if we called her husband and got him to come up and surprise the leader, paying for both of them to stay in the executive suite at camp for a couple of days? They had more than enough leaders in her cabin to be with the girls, and she could be with them and with her husband as well. What if?

I love the "What ifs" of life that can bring people hope! Somehow, I always want to look for the "what ifs." A "what if" dream,

What If?

a "what if" attitude change, a "what if" new perspective, a "what if" transformation, because Jesus is a "what if" God who desires to bring us "what if" hopes in the middle of our despairs, sorrows, and sacrifices, and even in the middle of death. All of this can happen because Jesus is alive.

Luke writes that Peter ran to look at the "what if" that the women were telling the truth? What if? Peter, as recorded in Luke 24:12, writes that he stooped in the tomb, looked in and saw, and then went home. By the way, the door of the tomb was only about three feet high, so he stooped and peered in. Then Peter would go in and see the linen wrappings lying alone, without the body of Jesus, and then he would leave to go home and wonder. Peter began to think about the impossible "what if."

Returning to my story, I asked the manager of the camp. We prayed about it, talked with her staff person, and then the "what if" happened. I called her husband and explained what we wanted to do, and he was so excited and astounded by the "what if" of him being paid to come up to camp and stay as our guest. He showed up and surprised her, and they spent two days and nights together. God gave the couple a blessed "what if."

Why do I write this story? I write this story because the risen Lord brings back into center focus the greatest of "what ifs"—for He who was once dead is now alive and desires to bless, bring, and breathe into us life.

"What if" I was healed of my abuse? "What if" we really did become new? "What if" Troy was right, and he really was going to be all right and be with Jesus? "What if" God was good, and all that seemed to be dark and broken in life will be redeemed and restored and made more than beautiful? "What if" we were made to be complete?

In Psalm 42, the deer pants for water and our souls pant for the living God. Why? Charles Spurgeon writes, "Because He lives, and gives to men the living water, therefore we with greater eagerness, desire Him. A dead God is a mere mockery; we loathe such a monstrous deity; but the ever-living God, the perennial fountain of life and light and love, is our soul's desire" (Spurgeon). So Peter begins to understand and to see with eyes of faith—to see for himself the "what ifs."

"What if" Jesus alive means the beginning of all "what ifs?" Oh, that we would take the time to listen and obey. The word "obey," in Greek, is *hupakouo*—"to come under one's voice" (Strong, 5219). There's a difference between hearing and listening: listening is a posture of humility and teachability, a surrendering of self, paying attention to the voice of God. Do you and I listen?

How will you listen to the Alive Jesus today? What will help you listen?

Jesus Alive meant the beginning of "what ifs." Jesus is the God who yearns for you to be restored.

"Oh, that the salvation of Israel would come out of Zion! When God restores His captive people, let Jacob rejoice, let Israel be glad" (Psalm 53:6).

Let us all be glad!

Jesus Christ—the God of "What Ifs!"

Scene (Seen) 26

A Seven-Mile Walk

Luke 24:13–18

And behold, two of them were going that very day to a village named Emmaus, which was about seven miles from Jerusalem. And they were talking with each other about all these things which had taken place. While they were talking and discussing, Jesus Himself approached and *began* traveling with them. But their eyes were prevented from recognizing Him. And He said to them, "What are these words that you are exchanging with one another as you are walking?" And they stood still, looking sad. One of them, named Cleopas, answered and said to Him, "Are You the only one visiting Jerusalem and unaware of the things which have happened here in these days?" (*NRSV*)

What gives you hope on an ordinary day? You begin your day and you end your day—how?

You make choices this day—choices of food, if you are so blessed; choices for reading and listening; choices as to who to respond to via phone, text, and social media; choices as to who to strive with and against; choices to hold on to and choices to let go of. Choices are made all day long; what helps you decide your choices?

What gives you hope?

Reading the Gospel of Luke: it was later in that day, when lives changed forever with the resurrection of Jesus, the day of First

Fruits. Women had come to tell the men what they had seen and heard; those men had choices. Some of them probably discussed the significance of this news as they scratched their heads with wonder. But they did not leave their house. Luke would record that Peter left for the tomb, and later, John would write that both of them left to check out the wildly imaginative story about the empty tomb. Two of the other men in the house just wanted to get away and go for a walk. You might have been like these men, one named Cleopas and the other not named. Maybe they had planned to go to Emmaus that day anyway. I like to imagine that these were the kind of guys that just couldn't sit still in the middle of their quarantine. They needed a break, some fresh air, and a chance to breathe, walk, and process.

Cleopas was the father of Matthew, the tax collector. Cleopas's wife was the other Mary mentioned in the Gospels, and maybe the sister-in-law of Mary, the mother of Jesus. Why does this matter? I think it is important for us to realize how very real these people are, how significant their story is, and how crucial it is to see that, like you and me, they were just people eating, breathing, and waiting for a break in the mundaneness of life. They had deep relationships yet gave one another enough space to be real in their frustrations and disappointments in life. Luke is recording real live people with real live issues, and the issue here is that none of the men believed; they refused to believe the women. Peter would question them and leave to go see for himself, but Cleopas and his friend proceeded to walk to Emmaus, seven miles away from Jerusalem. The seven-mile walk might be a necessary experience in the middle of confusion and anxiety; we all should give it a try!

What was that seven-mile walk like for Cleopas and his friend?

It was a walk filled with questions. The first question was asked by Jesus, although He was not recognized by the walkers—"Their eyes were prevented from recognizing Him." I wonder why it was that their eyes were prevented from recognizing Jesus? Was it because they were so involved in their own stories, consumed by the traumas of their own lives, and wrapped up in their own conversations? (If they had cellphones, they would have been just like us.) Is that why they were not able to see matters from a different perspective? Could they not recognize Jesus because Jesus looked different? Or was the reason they didn't know Him that they were not expecting Jesus? How about you and me?

> Are we so entangled in our own view, our own perceptions, our own stories, that we do not recognize Jesus? How do we become clear in our vision?

> Can you or I, by our own merits, bring clarity to the fog of following Jesus in this life?

Cleopas and his friend had to be interrupted by Jesus to become clear. And what did Jesus ask? He asked two questions. The first was, "What are these words that you are exchanging with one another as you are walking?" Jesus interrupts them on their seven-mile walk and doesn't sermonize to them, but instead chooses to listen to their stories! No doubt about it: Jesus longs to meet us and walk with us each day! They respond to Him with a tone that suggests incredulousness. In fact, with his humility gone out the window, Cleopas answers Jesus, "Are you the only one visiting Jerusalem and unaware of the things which have happened these days?" (Luke 24:18).

Let's just stop right there and get this straight. Two men who have just heard that Jesus is alive and the tomb is empty are walking seven miles to get a break—or maybe even just going to their favorite restaurant—and they are stopped by a stranger. The stranger is Jesus, only they don't recognize Him. Jesus asks them in-depth, wondering, completely perceptive questions. He had an attitude that was teachable. He had humility and listened. They, on the other hand, mocked this stranger in bold arrogance, saying, "Are you the only one?"

> When others are wanting to share their stories, their injustices, their confusions, or their perceptions, do you and I

take time to listen, care enough to ask, and, bottom-line, trust God enough to be genuine when fellow journeyers share their stories? How do you and I respond with impatience or patience?

Jesus, realizing their disbelief, asked them again, "What things?" I love the fact that Jesus asks them twice! He knows all, but He is patient, and I imagine He wants them to "get it off their chest."

The reason I know that He is not so quick to fix things is because of my own life. In my story, when I got my memories back, I could count four people in my life who cared enough to process with me my inward thoughts, my confusions, my terrors, and my sufferings. The rest wanted to try to fix me, to push me to the side, and to tell me to shape up, or just to dismiss me altogether. It takes time to love a person well; it's messy. Jesus takes the time to heal because He heals completely!

Do you or I take the time?

It makes sense, in this recording of Luke, that the image bearers didn't have the patience to listen, **but the Creator intentionally took the time to listen.**

Let's just pause right there and ask the Lord what questions He has for us today. Or maybe talk with Him about the ones you refused to listen to, and then go to them and ask for forgiveness. Take time to listen. We might not always agree with one another in the end, but we will be more understanding when we are more apt to listen to others and exercise patience. Who knows, we might even recognize—THE LIVING JESUS.

Jesus Christ—the God Who Patiently Listens and Completely Heals!

Scene (Seen) 27

A Cleopas Moment

Luke 24:19–24

And He said to them, "What things?" And they said to Him, "The things about Jesus the Nazarene, who was a prophet mighty in deed and word in the sight of God and all the people, and how the chief priests and our rulers delivered Him to the sentence of death, and crucified Him. But we were hoping that it was He who was going to redeem Israel. Indeed, besides all this, it is the third day since these things happened. But also some women among us amazed us. When they were at the tomb early in the morning, and did not find His body, they came, saying that they had also seen a vision of angels who said that He was alive. Some of those who were with us went to the tomb and found it just exactly as the women also had said; but Him they did not see." (*NRSV*)

*D*id you catch the name by which they called Jesus? Jesus the Nazarene is the name they chose to call Him. What could they have chosen to call Him? There were so many names they could have called Him: Jesus—son of Joseph, "Jesus who claimed to be God." But instead, they called Him Jesus the Nazarene. Nazareth was looked down on by important Jewish men. The disciple, Nathaniel, said this when he first met Jesus three years before: "Can any good thing come out of Nazareth?" (John 1:46). For those around Him, the vision of who Jesus was would be shaken to the core, turned upside down and inside out!

Has an inside-out transformation occurred in your life?

I remember the first night of waking up with a startled heart. I had what I thought was a terrible nightmare, which would reoccur over the weeks and months. I had completed about twenty years of ministry, and I had just returned from a youth camp. My nightmares became more and more detailed and repetitive, causing me to face the nights with dread. So, I called a counselor and asked to meet. I went for my appointment and sat down. I knew him a little, so I felt secure and told him about my nightmares. Then I told him that after my counseling classes in seminary, I was almost certain that I was projecting the stories of the kids that I spent time leading onto myself, and I just needed a break. I knew he would think that was accurate and right. I, like Cleopas, had my own scenario, my own perceptions, and honestly just wanted to be agreed with and get back to normal again.

The counselor listened patiently and proceeded to suggest, "Why don't we work through these nightmares for the next few weeks, and then I can give you tools to help you move through this time." I agreed, and for the next few weeks I met with him, assuredly believing that these were ministry-exhaustion projections. Self-diagnosis is always a dangerous thing.

One day, like this Cleopas day that we are reading about in Luke, my world was turned upside down and inside out when my counselor told me, "I can see you really have it all figured out. I can also see that you are a truth seeker, so I need to give it to you straight. Your nightmares are not just dreams; they are memories returning to you, and here are the ten clinical reasons why I believe this."

As I listened to his ten clinical reasons, my heart pounded in my ears, and my mind began to race and spin as I truly felt the weight of the reality of remembering begin to wrap around my chest, like chains around my heart and soul. I kept on wanting to scream that this wasn't true, and yet down in my soul I knew it was truer than I had ever wanted to hear.

It is costly to remember. One must trade a dream, a perspective of what one wishes, for a stark and brutal reality, and it left me with the question, "How can I live, knowing all of this? My life will be forever different! I cannot do this, and therefore I must not let go of what I think for this new perspective, even if it is true."

This is where my remembering showed me a place of desperate need for Jesus Christ in my soul, which was an awakened world of brokenness and abuse beyond what one can take as the daughter of the abuser—the one called dad in my life. Jesus had to hold me; that's all there was to it, and I was faced with a "Cleopas moment," like when he knew Jesus had to be real because his life was being flipped upside down! Jesus, alive Jesus, because nothing else will survive in my heart—nothing good, nothing beautiful, nothing worthy to live for—if Jesus were not alive.

God is good!

How can I say this in remembering the abuse, portion by portion? I can say this because as I close my eyes now, I can see those moments through the eyes of Jesus, who suffered at the hands of those He loved. Jesus is with me; He was with me then; He is with me now.

You might be asking, "How can you say that? Where is Jesus?" He lived inside me because as a child, I had asked Him to live in me and be my God. As a child, I had learned the story of Cleopas, and how he would remember and rehearse to the "stranger." I had heard that Jesus of Nazareth had healed the sick, fed the poor, set captives free, and then suffered, died on a cross, and came to life—not dead, but alive! He did all this for me and you, for my sin—selfishness—and my suffering, and for others' sin and selfishness, like the one who was my earthly father. After I told my father that I loved Jesus, as a child, the abuse would become even more difficult. So where was Jesus in my torment? He was in me, and I was able to endure because of His strength, and I was able to persevere because of His love, poured out on a cross for me. Not that I remembered that at the time—but I do believe He held me. I have a Father in heaven who is enough, and He sets me free. I am free to love, to live, and to walk through any news of any brokenness in my life, because Jesus loves me, and He is enough!

This is the same Jesus that Cleopas talks about remembering, when he talked with the "stranger" on that seven-mile walk. So no worries, all is well with my soul. How about yours? Can you take a seven-mile walk, talk to the One, and have a Cleopas moment? Maybe this Jesus has been a stranger to you, not because He chose it but because you chose it, and the world chose it for you. Well, this can all change in a Cleopas moment. Actively try to remember, because this is what Cleopas was doing. Or, hear for the first time that this Jesus is God, and He loves you. Cleopas recites the event, starting with his short-sighted vision of who Jesus was—Jesus of Nazareth.

No worries—remembering or hearing for the first time are not all that difficult, and Cleopas and his friend will not just be remembering the hard parts. Neither would I! Just as for these men on a seven-mile walk that would change them forever, there will be changes in our reasons for living, changes in our actual living, and changes with our families and friends forever. The reality of Christ would turn them upside down and inside out—into a transformational beauty that they would never dream possible! And this transformational beauty will happen to anyone who comes in contact with this Jesus of Nazareth. The reality of this Sacred Stranger would have the ability to cause them to flee from their avoidance, to flee from seeking numbness, and to press forward into the very presence of God their Creator—the stranger once, but now the Alive God of their hearts, minds, and souls. This Jesus will turn all of us upside down and inside out!

Is Jesus real in your life?

Is Jesus good?

Is Jesus in control?

Is Jesus love?

Is Jesus God?

They thought He was just Jesus of Nazareth; the surprise would be discovered.

Have you experienced inside out?

How do you see Jesus?

Jesus Christ—the God of Transformational Upside Down and Inside Out!

Scene (Seen) 28

Necessary to Suffer

Luke 24:25–27

And He said to them, "O foolish men and slow of heart to believe in all that the prophets have spoken! Was it not necessary for the Christ to suffer these things and to enter into His glory?" Then beginning with Moses and with all the prophets, He explained to them the things concerning Himself in all the Scriptures. (*NRSV*)

Jesus asked three questions, with two points, of Cleopas and his friend. The first two questions were, "What are these words that you are exchanging with one another as you are walking?" and, again later, he would ask, "What things?" (Luke 24:17, 19). The questions, I imagine, were asked by Jesus to help Cleopas and his friend to slow down and process the events and remember. Sometimes all of us move too quickly to our perspectives without taking into account the details. How did Cleopas respond? He responded by listing these facts:

1. They called him Jesus of Nazareth.
2. Jesus was a prophet, mighty in deed and word, in the sight of God and all the people.
3. Jesus was delivered by the chief priest and rulers.
4. Jesus was delivered a sentence of death.
5. Jesus was crucified.

Necessary to Suffer

6. Cleopas stated he had been hoping it was Jesus who would redeem Israel, and now, obviously, that wasn't going to happen.
7. It was the third day, and some women among them went to the tomb early and couldn't find His body.
8. The women said they saw a vision of angels who said He was alive.
9. Some of their friends went to the tomb, and it was exactly how the women had said.
10. But they did not see Jesus.

So, reader, did you know that in Luke 24, there are three times that Luke wrote about what Jesus came to do for them? He wrote that Jesus Christ would be delivered by sinful men, crucified, and rise again on the third day:

1. By angels—Luke 24:7
2. By Jesus Himself on the road to Emmaus—Luke 24:25–27
3. By Jesus' appearance to the disciples in the room—Luke 24:46–48

Over 183 times, people ask Jesus questions. In Luke, Jesus asks over eighty-five questions, either in His stories or directly. Jesus used questions to make His point in teaching. Think about this question: If you were Cleopas or his friend, and Jesus was asking you the question, "Was it not necessary for the Christ to suffer these things and to enter into His glory," why would Jesus be asking this unless He wanted to make a point? What was the point? His point was that He had to suffer all these things, and He had to enter into His glory. One doesn't stand alone. Both were necessary. Why would Jesus have to suffer to the point of death? The friend of Luke, Paul, would later write in his letter to the Romans (5:6–10):

> For while we were still helpless, at the right time Christ died for the ungodly. For one will hardly die for a righteous man; though perhaps for the good man someone would dare even

to die. 8 But God demonstrates His own love toward us, in that while we were yet sinners, Christ died for us. Much more then, having now been justified by His blood, we shall be saved from the wrath of God through Him. For if while we were enemies we were reconciled to God through the death of His Son, much more, having been reconciled, we shall be saved by His life. And not only this, but we also exult in God through our Lord Jesus Christ, through whom we have now received the reconciliation.

Jesus suffered to understand your sufferings, my sufferings, others' sufferings. Even greater than this, Jesus not only pays for my sin, but through His coming to life—His entering His glory—you and I have the promise of life forever, with, in, and through Jesus.

Cleopas and his friend had no answer for Jesus, so Jesus answered for them. "Then beginning with Moses and with all the prophets, He explained to them the things concerning Himself in all the Scriptures." (I wonder how many miles they had walked before meeting Jesus on the road, asking him, and then rather mockingly listening to him as he explained the Scriptures?) The walk must have been delightful, and definitely not boring! Jesus would be walking and talking about the beautiful and grace-filled future of the Christ, the Messiah, the Lord of Hosts, Elohim, Prince of Peace, Great Counselor, and Almighty God.

Now Jesus will hide no longer. He will reveal his sine cera (*Sincerely Seen*) self, and Cleopas and his friend will never be the same! They will indeed be transformed into sine cera (*Sincerely Seen*) people, following the Sine Cera God. He will be seen sincerely.

Take time now to read Isaiah 9:2–7 and imagine Jesus the Nazarene explaining this to them, and explaining it to you and me.

What are you thinking? How can you learn to be more vulnerable, more real, and more sincerely alive with Jesus and with others?

Jesus Christ the Nazarene.

Scene (Seen) 29

Remember

Luke 24:28

And they approached the village where they were going, and He acted as though He were going farther. (NRSV)

The friends of Jesus were challenged to remember who Jesus is, what Jesus did, and that Jesus is alive. Remember!

What do you remember now of what the Gospel writers have explained to you of Jesus' story—<u>His</u>tory?

It's human nature for your mind to drift into your own story while you are remembering Jesus' story. Why? Because the story of Jesus is about God showing up in the story of humanity, past, present, and future. That's what Jesus Christ, the Nazarene, fully man and fully God, is all about: showing up in our stories, with no hesitation about the mess!

So—my encouragement to you, as you are thinking through His story, is this: when you drift into thinking of your story, lay it down and say out loud, "Welcome, Father God. Welcome, Son of God. Welcome, Holy Spirit." Then envision Jesus, and lay in His hands your very own story, past, present, and future, and get back to His story. YOU WILL BE SURPRISED at the benefit to your heart, mind, and soul, and with others around you! Your attitude about the little things, and even the great things, will begin to take a humble step into the light of welcoming Jesus Christ and His story into your life. I know my expectations for myself and others become lighter when I focus on Jesus Christ's story. When you or I lay our stories in His nail-scarred hands, His very alive hands, the ones that broke bread after He died and ate with His friends, then our focus becomes less about self. Our priorities will shift, and everything might become clearer and lighter in perspective. "It would often do our souls a world of good to make a pilgrimage to the place where we first found God" (Barclay, 79). I would say, "It does my soul good to remember that God found me when I was lost, at great cost to Himself, and He promises never to let go!"

What are you and I waiting for? When we come to the place where we first found God (or rather, He first found us), there is such joy. When we become engulfed in our stories—stop and remember. Remember who Jesus is, and what Jesus has done, and how Jesus is alive. Remember.

Jesus Christ—God Who Finds!

Scene (Seen) 30

Sacred Meal

Luke 24:29–30

But they urged Him, saying, "Stay with us, for it is getting toward evening, and the day is now nearly over." So He went in to stay with them. When He had reclined at the table with them, He took the bread and blessed it, and breaking it. He began giving *it* to them. (*NRSV*)

Jesus stayed with Cleopas and his friend that early evening. Whom do you invite to dinner? Is it only your family and friends? Why do we invite the ones we invite to a meal?

*I*s it out of love, or out of what we can get out of a situation? **A meal is sacred.** I have fed one, and I have fed hundreds. I have fed friends, strangers, and even those who have hurt me in the past and present, and who probably will do so again in the future. There is something "magical" that happens in a heart as one prepares a meal for another, especially an enemy.

The Scriptures contain countless stories of people preparing meals for family, friends, and enemies, from Genesis through Revelation. The meal has a primary place in relationships. The lack of a meal has also been recorded in the scriptures: famines. Famines and meals are incredibly significant. Examples of these famines and meals are many. In the Old Testament, there are the famines that brought Israel to Joseph in Egypt, where forgiveness and reconciliation would be the end result. Then there was the first Passover meal, recorded in Exodus, which would set in motion the freedom of the thousands of Jews being oppressed by Egypt. The New Testament records the first miracle of Jesus occurring at a wedding feast. The story of Mary and Martha feeding Jesus is in Luke 10.

There are stories throughout all of the Gospels about Jesus Himself preparing meals for thousands—healing and filling! One of the key recorded stories is when Jesus prepared the feast of Passover, washed the feet of His disciples, and proclaimed a new covenant with the Passover bread and cup of wine. The Holy Spirit would complete His own feast (not necessarily a meal, but they were definitely filled by God's Spirit) with the representatives of all the nations on the day of Pentecost! And last, but really at the beginning of the age to come, there is the meal that will occur when the Father invites the ones who follow Jesus to the "marriage supper of the Lamb" (Rev. 19:9)! So the question today is:

Who is the Lord challenging you to prepare for, to sit down and have a meal with today? Remember His words in Matt.25:34-45:

Then the King will say to those on His right, "Come, you who are blessed of My Father, inherit the kingdom prepared for you from the foundation of the world. For I was hungry, and you gave Me something to eat; I was thirsty, and you gave Me something to drink; I was a stranger, and you invited Me in; naked, and you clothed Me; I was sick, and you visited Me; I was in prison, and you came to Me." Then the righteous will answer Him, "Lord, when did we see You hungry, and feed You, or thirsty, and give You something to drink? And when did we see You a stranger, and invite You in, or naked, and clothe You? When did we see You sick, or in prison, and come to You?" The King will answer and say to them, "Truly I say to you, to the extent that you did it to one of these brothers of Mine, even the least of them, you did it to Me." Then He will also say to those on His left, "Depart from Me, accursed ones, into the eternal fire which has been prepared for the devil and his angels; for I was hungry, and you gave Me nothing to eat; I was thirsty, and you gave Me nothing to drink; I was a stranger, and you did not invite Me in; naked, and you did not clothe Me; sick, and in prison, and you did not visit Me." (*NSRV*)

You might be asking the question, "How do I prepare a meal for or sit down with my enemy at a meal?" I understand. By myself, it's impossible, but with Christ—and remember, Christ is with you—it is possible:

1. Examine your heart.
2. See your bitterness, anger, and malice.
3. Confess to Jesus.
4. Receive Jesus' love while you have this heart.
5. Truth will be necessary; Love is essential.
6. All in Christ: Love plus Truth equals Grace.
7. Then get up, serve, and eat with them.

It takes many a meal to work through the hearts of longing and hearts of pain and loneliness. It takes courage and self-denial. But you can do it in Christ, with eyes on Christ. And of course:

8. Don't forget to "Say Grace!"

Jesus Christ— the God Who Prepares a Feast!

Scene (Seen) 31

Cooking for the King

Luke 24:30–32

When He had reclined at the table with them, He took the bread and blessed it, and breaking it, He *began* giving *it* to them. Then their eyes were opened and they recognized Him; and He vanished from their sight. They said to one another, "Were not our hearts burning within us while He was speaking to us on the road, while He was explaining the Scriptures to us?" (*NRSV*)

So, did you prepare the meal and eat with the ones Jesus asked you to eat with, after Scene (Seen) 30? Not yet? Then stop reading and get started. Write about that time, and when you have finished, trust me, it will be good:Can you imagine Cleopas and company as they sit unknowingly with the King of Kings, and Jesus blesses bread, breaks bread, and bestows bread upon their plates? It reminds me of something Jesus said to His disciples: "Truly I say to you, to the extent that you did not do it to one of the least of these, you did not do it to Me" (Matt. 25:45).

Cleopas and his friend ask the age-old question of the ones who sat with nobility, "Were not our hearts burning within us while He was speaking with us on the road, while He was explaining the Scriptures to us?" (Luke 24:32). Notice that their hearts burned as Jesus explained the Scriptures. I have another question:

Cooking for the King

When you read the Scriptures about meals, as the question about eating with enemies was asked, didn't your heart burn within you?

No worries, I sit in company with you, if that is any consolation. The word "burn," in Luke 24:32, means "To set on fire, light, burning" (Strong, 2544). Just like yours, my heart burns, and my mind won't shut off when there is a task to which Jesus challenges me. You are not alone.

The most amazing part of this story is this: "Then their eyes were opened and they recognized Him; and He vanished from their sight." Their eyes were opened when they ate the bread that Jesus gave to them—when they received from Him. And isn't it ironic that this Jesus, who had been betrayed, passively or aggressively, by all—including Cleopas and his friend—was now there with them, and He was feeding them? Jesus was feeding them a meal— his friends, the ones who stayed low and quiet when He was being crucified, not showing up to help Him or risk for Him. Jesus was feeding them!

Your eyes and mine will be opened to Jesus showing up alive when we sit down with the stranger, the alien, the oppressed, the poor, the broken, the needy, and eat with them—not just feed them and tower over them, but sit down with them and enjoy a meal together and get to know them face-to-face, eye-to-eye, soul-to-soul. Our eyes will see Jesus alive as never before. It is then that we will all see Jesus, as He shows us our own needs, our own oppressors and oppressions, our own hungers and thirsts, our own brokenness, our own angers, our own bitterness, our own prejudices, and our own deep-rooted pains. Then we are all at the table as one, feeding each other.

There is an example of heaven and hell with which I would like to close this devotion. It's an allegory written so long ago that no one really knows the author. It goes something like this:

> One day a man said to God, "God, I would like to know what heaven and hell are like." God showed the man two doors.

Inside the first one, in the middle of the room, was a large table with a large pot of vegetable stew. It smelled delicious and made the man's mouth water, but the people sitting around the table were thin. They appeared to be famished. They were holding spoons with very long handles, and each found it possible to reach into the pot of stew and take a spoonful, but because the handles were longer than their arms, they could not get the spoons with stew into their own mouths. The man shuddered at the sight of their misery and suffering. God said, "You have seen Hell."

Behind the second door, the room appeared exactly as the first room. There was the large round table with the large pot of wonderful vegetable stew that made the man's mouth water. The people had the same long-handled spoons, but the people were well rounded and plump and laughing and talking and enjoying one another. The man said, "I don't understand." God smiled. "It is simple." He said, "Love only requires one skill. These people learned early on to share and feed one another, while the others were greedy and only thinking of themselves." The man looked and he saw that indeed, the people were feeding each other. They were able to get spoons of food and then feed each other. Community loving one another.

Now we know heaven and hell are not about our works: "For by grace you have been saved through faith; and that not of yourselves, *it is* the gift of God; not as a result of works, so that no one may boast" (Eph. 2:8–9).

For the last six years, one of the greatest joys of my life, besides my amazing family, is serving my Latino brothers and sisters (my high school friends), who would come to eat dinner at my house every other week. Many times, it was hard work coming home from teaching all day and then making dinner for fifty to sixty kids and their leaders. But every time I did it, as I prepared and swept the porch and cooked the meal, I would pray and tell myself, "I am cooking for the KING." That's the truth. When we serve others, we serve the KING.

The question I have is, "Would Cleopas and company have seen Jesus alive if they hadn't sat down and let Jesus feed them?" We are all in need of a Savior; we all sit at the table in need, "for all have sinned and fall short of the glory of God" (Rom. 3:23). So, what will you do to see Jesus around the next corner? I want to recognize my need for Jesus, let Him feed me, and then join Him as He feeds others.

What do you want?

Christ Jesus—the King!

Scene (Seen) 32

Seven-Mile Run!

Luke 24:31–35

Then their eyes were opened and they recognized Him; and He vanished from their sight. They said to one another, "Were not our hearts burning within us while He was speaking to us on the road, while He was explaining the Scriptures to us?" And they got up that very hour and returned to Jerusalem, and found gathered together the eleven and those who were with them, saying, "The Lord has really risen and has appeared to Simon." They began to relate their experiences on the road and how He was recognized by them in the breaking of the bread. (*NRSV*)

What happened as Jesus broke the bread?

How did the two men respond? What could they have done? What did they choose to do?

When you experienced Christ in your story, what was your first response?

What questions do you have from reading this?

The question I have always thought of when I read this, "Why did Jesus disappear right when they recognized Him?" It seems to me that He would want to take some moments while eating to talk about what happened and who He was, and to let Cleopas and friend soak it up.

Maybe there wasn't a moment to lose. Jesus is God, Jesus is

alive, and He didn't want to field questions. He has a plan: to go to Galilee. Remember? He told the women, "Come and see, go quickly, and tell My disciples to proceed to Galilee. There they will see Me" (Matt. 28:10). In all the stories of Jesus' resurrection, there is no record of days upon days of Jesus hanging around with the folks and teaching, like he did before He went to the cross—before He was glorified.

Did you know that the word "glorified" has two meanings in the Hebrew language. It means beauty or it means "weight" in the Hebrew language. When God's glory comes down, it is those present who are able to see the weight, the grand importance compared to all else created, of He who is: King of Kings, God—YHWH—I Am Who Am—Elohim. He is higher than all creation. He is unsurpassable beauty. He is more important than any created thing on this earth.

Jesus would talk about Himself being glorified many times. Here are just a few references: John 7:39, 12:19, and 23. He who is fully man and fully God laid down His life to the point of dying on a cross so that He might pay the penalty for my sin and yours. Why would you or I have a penalty for our sin? Well, sin is an expression of missing the mark in archery—missing the bullseye. Speaking only for myself, I know that when I sin, I am missing the mark—the bullseye—of who I was made to be. The cause of my sin is usually my own selfishness, my wanting to do things my way. Sometimes when I see the word sin, I actually think of it as "sIn," with the "I" in the middle capitalized, because when I "sIn," I make things all about me. There is no room for anyone else when I make things all about myself, and thus the consequences of my sin are broken relationships with those who are the recipients of my selfishness.

Now, placing this in the realm of a relationship with God, the consequence of my sin is a broken relationship. And since I sin all the time (whether in mind or in action), I have a constant broken relationship with God. It's as if there is a death in my relationship with God. And because I cannot be perfect, as God is perfect, I am left with this broken relationship forever. **EXCEPT** for God's glory! God so longs for a right relationship with me, you, and all people that He chose to permanently change this brokenness. The penalty or the consequence of sin is separation from God, so God decided to take on my penalty and your penalty, my consequence and your consequence, by taking on the fullness of death (or separation). He is the Great Rescue. He is the Victorious One. He is the Perfect Remedy for my plight, which is separation from God.

When Jesus died on the cross, He cried out, "It is finished." What was finished? My consequence—your consequence—of death and separation from God was finished. The Father's weight (His glory) would be magnified to the extreme for all humanity as He took on our failures in relationship with Him. He would give up His Son as the full payment for you and me. My need and your need were traded by the One who would make us whole and fulfilled, complete and restored, when He voluntarily went to the cross and experienced the fullness of my brokenness and yours, including our separation from God, our thirst for God, our desperateness for God. In His dying, I am made one with God as I receive this great Glory-Gift. Then, in His rising, I am raised up with Him for all eternity. Jesus was glorified that you and I might have life, and have it abundantly. No wonder Jesus left Cleopas and his friend quickly. Many people needed to hear the good news—that Jesus was and is alive. Cleopas and his friend left quickly, just like the women—notice the words, "And they got up that very hour and returned to Jerusalem."

Now, it was a SEVEN-MILE RUN. They ran back to Jerusalem, no longer tired, no longer weary, no longer grieving, and no longer confused. They were no longer depressed, no longer anxious, and no longer floundering in bewilderment. Glory was abounding—the weight of being freed for a relationship with God was theirs! They had a purpose, to go and tell. No wonder they ran. There was not a moment to lose—not one moment!

Remember your story, and remember when you realized that Jesus died for you, that the nails in His hands were taken for you.

Seven-Mile Run!

Remember Jesus is alive, not dead. That very news means that we will not stay dead. We will rise again.

> In My Father's house are many dwelling places; if it were not so, I would have told you; for I go to prepare a place for you. If I go and prepare a place for you, I will come again and receive you to Myself, so that where I am, there you may be also. (John 14:2-3)

Now don't just sit there, my friends, my brothers and sisters in the Lord. Go and tell your friends. There's not a moment to lose. List the names of people you need to go to and tell this news, and then do it. It's the new Seven-Mile Run—Marathon!

Jesus Christ—Our Great Rescue!

Scene (Seen) 33

An AHA Moment!

Luke 24:36–43

While they were telling these things, He Himself stood in their midst and said to them, "Peace be to you." But they were startled and frightened and thought that they were seeing a spirit. And He said to them, "Why are you troubled, and why do doubts arise in your hearts? See My hands and My feet, that it is I Myself; touch Me and see, for a spirit does not have flesh and bones as you see that I have." And when He had said this, He showed them His hands and His feet. While they still could not believe it because of their joy and amazement, He said to them, "Have you anything here to eat?" They gave Him a piece of a broiled fish; and He took it and ate *it* before them. (*NRSV*)

What are the most astounding, literally unbelievable moments you have ever had? You know, your AHA moments. Write about them:

Now, after writing this—or for those who don't like to write, after thinking about this—what was most astounding for you, and how did it affect you?

I have been blessed by many such astounding moments, when I knew, "That couldn't have been a coincidence!" My list is many:

Babies born—Four incredible sons!
Loving and serving young people by the thousands!
Detailed prayers fulfilled.

An AHA Moment!

An example was when I found out that my grandmother was sick, and I flew to a little town to be with her. I had prayed, "Lord, help me to get to her tonight, to the little Guadalupe Hospital, and may she have a Christian doctor and nurse who care for her." I flew to Albuquerque, and then I was able to get on a small "puddle jumper" plane with only twenty seats. I got off the plane in the small town of Carlsbad, New Mexico, around 10:00 p.m. A few people got off and got in their cars immediately. I looked around to see if I could call a cab, back before cell phones or Ubers, but it was a tiny airport. So I went inside, where I saw the pilot grab his bag and go to shut off the airport office lights. I realized then that the pilot was also the airport management. I told you it was small!

I asked him, "Sir, is there a phone around here that I can use to call a taxi?" The man laughed and said, "Ma'am, we're not like the city; we're a small town," as he kept turning off the lights. I saw two elderly women standing nearby, talking to each other as they were looking at the plane. They were shaking their heads and saying, "I guess the package didn't come." And then they asked the pilot, "Excuse me, did you have a package for Guadalupe Hospital?" He shook his head, said no, and got ready to walk out the door. I stood there, shocked, remembering my detailed prayer, thinking all the more, could it be that God wants me to go with them?

I said to them, "Excuse me, are you going to Guadalupe Hospital?"

And they answered, "Well, we came to get a package for that hospital. There are only two hospitals in our town, but we were told to bring the package to Guadalupe. But the package didn't come. Why?"

I stood there wondering if I should say anything. I have always had a hard time asking for things for myself or being assertive for my own needs. Grabbing the courage, I said to the two kind, older ladies, who wearing long coats like they were bundled up for November weather, "Well, my grandmother is sick and in ICU at Guadalupe Hospital, and I need to get there. I thought I could get a taxi, but the airport is closing down, and I don't know how to get there. Could you give me a ride?"

One of the dear ladies said, "Oh, honey, there are no taxis in Carlsbad this late at night. But we will take you." I put my suitcase in the trunk and got in their car. It took about twenty minutes to get there because the airport was out of town. Once we got there, they said to me, "We will help you to your grandmother." And they grabbed the suitcase and walked ahead of me all the way to the ICU. I saw a sign above the door that said, "Please push button to notify the nursing station." I did so, and then turned around to thank the two kind women who had helped me, but they weren't there, so I ran down the small hallway and out the door of the hospital to say thank you and offer to pay them something. That is when the AHA moment occurred. THEY WERE NOT THERE! There were no little old ladies, no car, nothing in sight.

I went to the information desk and asked the gentleman who was sitting there watching television, "Did you see two women walk out?" And he said, "Nope. No one has come out for a long time. I saw them come in with you. Do you need help?" "No thanks," I said, bewildered. I looked for the ladies frantically, thinking to myself, "Am I going crazy?" There were no more entrances in the hospital, so I looked out at the parking lot one more time, then returned to the ICU. The ICU nurse was standing there looking at my suitcase, and I walked up and told her I was here to see my grandmother.

She said, "Well, normally we don't let anyone in after visiting hours, but it's slow tonight, and you've come from out of town, so come on in and you can be with her."

I was able to spend that night with her, the very last night of her life before she went to be with the Alive Jesus. I sang to her, held her hand, prayed for her, and just had a night of quietly sitting next to her. The doctor came up to me, introduced himself, and asked where I was from. I told him how I had come from Phoenix to be with my dear Grandmother. He saw my Bible in my lap as I was holding her arm, and he said, "Love that book! I have

An AHA Moment!

one I carry with me all the time," patting his clinic jacket pocket. He had a small pocket Bible. Then I remembered my two prayers: "Lord, help me to get to my grandmother, and may she have a Christian doctor who cares for her."

As I sat there in that second AHA moment, I told him how thankful I was for him. He told me, "You are really calm and peaceful, so you can stay here with her as long as you want."

Was it a coincidence? No! Not at all! Who were those women? I don't know! Either they can read this story and let me know it was them so that I can thank them, or maybe they were God's sent angels! I mean, two "men" showed up at Jesus' tomb to tell the women! God could have female angels too! Either way, it was an AHA moment when I discovered the space between heaven and earth seemed a little bit closer to me!

This story of Luke 24:36–43 was definitely an AHA moment for all the disciples except the one who wasn't there, Thomas! It was such an AHA moment that Jesus would tell His friends to touch His hands and feet, and then eat some broiled fish—all to help them come out of the fog of disbelief and into the clarity that HE IS ALIVE. No wonder Jesus' words were, "Peace be with you." I don't blame His friends! I think they felt as I did when I ran out to find that the women had vanished. It's the same feeling I had as I held my beloved grandmother's hands as the doctor patted his Bible.

> **What about you? Have you had an AHA moment? The Lord has many AHA moments for His children. I think if we were to take the time to share them, we might be more joy-filled, more abundantly joyful, and more kind and loving to one another.**
>
> **Peace be with you. And then I pray: AHA be with you!**

Jesus Christ—the Master of AHA!

Scene (Seen) 34

Merry Christmas... Even If It's Not!

Luke 24:44–53

Then he said to them, "These are my words that I spoke to you while I was still with you—that everything written about me in the law of Moses, the prophets, and the psalms must be fulfilled." Then he opened their minds to understand the scriptures, and he said to them, "Thus it is written, that the Messiah is to suffer and to rise from the dead on the third day, and that repentance and forgiveness of sins is to be proclaimed in his name to all nations, beginning from Jerusalem. You are witnesses of these things. And see, I am sending upon you what my Father promised; so stay here in the city until you have been clothed with power from on high." Then he led them out as far as Bethany, and, lifting up his hands, he blessed them. While he was blessing them, he withdrew from them and was carried up into heaven. And they worshiped him, and returned to Jerusalem with great joy; and they were continually in the temple blessing God. (*NRSV*)

This would be the third history lesson Jesus' followers would be given that day, but this one was so much more detailed. Jesus, after eating with His friends, begins with the Law of Moses, discussing the Prophets and the Psalms (oh, to hear Jesus talk about the Psalms...yes, please!) and telling His followers what?

Make a list of what Jesus tells His friends, and let it sink into your heart. What was the most impactful word to you? Why do you think Jesus brought up these points when He could have spoken about anything?

List:

1. Jesus reminds His friends that what occurred the past few days was written in the Law of Moses, the Prophets and the Psalms. Here are three examples:

> Law of Moses: Lev. 17:11–12
> Prophets: Isa. 53
> Psalms: Ps. 22

According to the Law of Moses, blood needs to be shed for atonement of sin. The word atonement in the Hebrew, that Jesus is quoting, is the word, *kaphar. This Hebrew word means:* "to cover, purge, make reconciliation, to cancel, cleanse, forgive, pardon" (Strong, G3722). Moses would write in Leviticus that there must be blood shed for there to be a covering of one's sin. Why would it be important to Jesus to share this particular Scripture? Jesus is explaining that His blood shed will be the ultimate covering so as to make those who believe be one with God. He was telling His friends how there was a need for One to die for all men and women, a blood sacrifice, a life given for the many. I always think of *kaphar* as "at-one-ment" with God.

Then He uses the Prophets to proclaim who He is, quoting Isaiah 53. So, pause for a moment, and read this quote:

> Peter Stoner, in his classic book *Science Speaks*, calculated the chance of any man fulfilling these prophecies, even down to the present time, to be 1 in 100,000,000,000,000,000 (10 to the 17th power). How can anyone think that Jesus just "happened" to be in the right place at the right time? Clearly, we can't consider coincidence. To help us visually comprehend the staggering odds of this probability, Stoner proposed that

we take that many silver dollars and lay them across the state of Texas. In doing so, we'd find they would stack up across the state two feet deep. But wait; there's more! Now mark one of the silver dollars, and stir up the entire mass of coins. Then blindfold an enthusiastic volunteer and tell him that he can travel as far as he likes across Texas, but that he *must• pick out the marked silver dollar. THAT is how difficult it would be for one man to fulfill these prophecies. *Unless, of course, he did so because of divine appointment.* (McDowell Ministries, Peter Stoner)

This helps us to understand the probabilities of eight prophecies, let alone over three hundred prophecies, being fulfilled by just one person. These are the odds. Jesus would speak to his friends about the Prophets pointing to Him. And then, there are the Psalms. The Psalms point to Jesus; look at Psalm 22. It would speak of crucifixion, and there was no such torture at the time that Psalm was written. Yet there it is, plainly: "For dogs have surrounded me; A band of evildoers has encompassed me; They pierced my hands and my feet. I can count all my bones. They look, they stare at me; They divide my garments among them, And for my clothing they cast lots" (Pss. 22:16–18).

Jesus was lifting the veil of disbelief from the eyes of His doubters because He valued their questions, their doubts, and their fears.

What questions or doubts do you have? Going back to our list:

2. **Jesus tells His friends: it was written that the Christ would suffer.**
3. **It was written the Christ would rise from the dead on the third day.**
4. **It was written that forgiveness of sins would be proclaimed in Christ's name to all the nations. (Not just Israel.)**

5. Jesus told them He would be sending forth the Promise of His Father upon them. (God's Spirit is His promise!)
6. Jesus told them to stay in the city until they were clothed (covered) with power on high.

This was Dr. Luke's sermon, never preached, just talked about. What Jesus said was that Scripture proclaimed it all: Christ's suffering, Christ's rising, forgiveness through Christ, the clothing of power on high, God's Spirit. Let's put it in practical terms: The God who created all, who knows every star, every person, every ocean, every cell, everything great and small, wrote a book to tell you and me about the One who would come and suffer for you and me unto actual death, and then rise again to be alive. Why? For my need of forgiveness and for yours, God demands holiness, and we do not have it. He would provide the One who would be like us in all things but distraction from God (sin), and who would pay the penalty of that distraction from God—life without God, the consequence of me choosing not to be with God. Christ experienced the fullness of my distraction from God. The God who created all, and is our All in All, wants to cover you and me with the payment He made in His Son.

Random story: One Christmas, we decided to get our four sons a puppy. We wrapped a box, first the bottom and then the lid, placed the puppy in the box early on Christmas morning, and put it under the tree. The boys came in and began to look through their individual piles, as they had been accustomed to do, when they entered the Christmas-tree room. One of my sons, Daniel, heard a little "yelp" from the box and walked over to it. He was staring at it when he heard a yelp again, and then he called his brothers over to come check it out. Two of the boys joined him, and they opened the box lid to see a puppy looking at them.

Delighted, they were quiet in their excitement, recognizing that they didn't want to frighten the puppy. Daniel, the first finder, had picked up the puppy and was holding him in his arms. With hushed voices, they were oohing and ahhing over the dog, but our other son, David, was so engrossed in his snare drum that he didn't even know what was happening. He was stroking his drum, picking up the drumsticks, and his back was totally to his brothers.

Finally, after they called for David to come and see a couple of times (and him not hearing them), he finally turned around and saw the joy of what they had—a LIVE present! Nothing can compare to a present that is ALIVE! David instantly dropped his drumsticks and ran to hold this LIVE gift, and they all sat together in a beautiful moment, letting the LIVE gift soak into their hearts and minds. Their lives would be different, and they had a LIVE friend to be with them, as illustrated by their leaving the room full of gifts—all else didn't matter—and they went outside to play with and delight in their LIVE gift.

I think this was what it was like as Jesus said those words, those Scriptures, to His friends after eating with them. He let the news soak into them, and then the joy. Oh, the joy that must have been in that room as He told them that they would receive power from on high! Their lives, always and forever, would be completely changed as they celebrated their ALIVE gift, Jesus Christ. Today, celebrate your LIVE Jesus Christ. Look at the Law, the Prophets, and the Psalms, and celebrate. No wonder Luke ended with Luke 24:50–53:

"Then he led them out as far as Bethany, and, lifting up his hands, he blessed them. While he was blessing them, he withdrew from them and was carried up into heaven. And they worshiped him, and returned to Jerusalem with great joy; and they were continually in the temple blessing God."

They went to celebrate the ALIVE Christ in their backyards in Jerusalem; they immediately left to go back. Who would do anything else? As the theologian William Barclay writes, "The Christian goes onwards, not to a night which fails, but to a dream which breaks" (Barclay).

So—what's that to you or me? Remember, Repent and Be empowered by God. He has promised us IT ALL—The ALIVE

Jesus. The promise of a life that is not just forgiven but eternal, with all those who follow Him, with a glorified body like His and a full, completely satisfying life with the God of Creation and Beyond.

I know it may not be Christmas as you read this. In fact, as I write this, it is not—but then, wait. Christmas, the celebration of Christ, should be an everyday occurrence because Jesus is with us. He is Emmanuel; God with us! One of the great challenges of my life is to look at each day as Christmas. So, with that attitude, I wish you today, a MERRY CHRISTMAS!

Jesus Christ—
God of Christmas Joy Forever!

Scene (Seen) 35

The Eagle's Review

First off: Who was John, and what do you know?

He was a fisherman with his brother, James; they were the sons of Zebedee. His father, who was a fisherman, might have been named Thunder, or possibly his sons were called Thunder, by Jesus: *Boanerges*, which is Greek for thunder.

Either way, the family had a reputation. Maybe their father was a powerful, booming-voiced man, and the manner in which John and James are described is by the reputation of their father. Or maybe, James and John were the thunderous sons. Dr. Luke mentions that when the brothers were traveling with Jesus, some village people wouldn't let them stay in the village. "When James and John saw this, they said to Jesus, 'Lord, should we call down fire from heaven to burn them up?'" But Jesus turned and rebuked them. "So they went on to another village" (Luke 9:54). They very well could have been the loud, in-charge, and vengeful type.

Now, whatever the reason for this thunderous description, these two had been invited to follow Jesus by Jesus Himself a little earlier: "Jesus saw two other brothers, James and John, sitting in a boat with their father, Zebedee, repairing their nets. And he called them to come with Him. They immediately followed him, leaving the boat and their father behind" (Matt. 4:21–22).

John was faster than Peter in running, and maybe even faster in believing that Jesus was God; we will see this in his story. John would write with an eagle's view; he was able to see the big picture, as an eagle soars through the heavens and glides over the lakes. Yet in one quick flash, the eagle is able to spot from on high a fish swimming in a lake, and he can swoop down with precision to scoop that tiny fish up with his talons.

John is able to see the details of the Christ encounters. John is also able to see the greater picture of the Lord Jesus as the mighty fulfillment of the Trinity's plan of salvation. John swoops down in his writings to choose only seven signs (out of the many that Jesus performed) in order to feed his hungry reader with an accurate picture of who Jesus is and what He would say about Himself, His Father who art in heaven, and the Holy Spirit. John would be the author of Revelation as well. Notice that John gives us not a bunch of revelations, but only one Revelation: the yet-to-come Kingdom on earth, as it is in heaven! I begin this last section of the stories of the resurrection with a scripture from Revelation 21:3-7:

> I heard a loud shout from the throne, saying, "Look, God's home is now among his people! He will live with them, and they will be his people. God himself will be with them. He will wipe every tear from their eyes, and there will be no more death or sorrow or crying or pain. All these things are gone forever." And the one sitting on the throne said, "Look, I am making everything new!" And then he said to me, "Write this down, for what I tell you is trustworthy and true." And he also said, "It is finished! I am the Alpha and the Omega—the Beginning and the End. To all who are thirsty I will give freely from the springs of the water of life. All who are victorious will inherit all these blessings, and I will be their God, and they will be my children." (*NRSV*).

What encouragement do you receive from reading this profound vision?

How have you seen Jesus coming around the next corner of your life?

Jesus Christ—the Alpha and the Omega— the Beginning and the End

Scene (Seen) 36

Wrapped Up in Sine Cera–ity.

John 20:1–2

Early on the first day of the week, while it was still dark, Mary Magdalene came to the tomb and saw that the stone had been removed from the tomb. So she ran and went to Simon Peter and the other disciple, the one whom Jesus loved, and said to them, "They have taken the Lord out of the tomb, and we do not know where they have laid him." (*NRSV*)

John was all about personal stories. He wrapped his final two Gospel chapters around five specific people: Jesus, Mary Magdalene, Thomas, Peter, and himself, "the disciple whom Jesus loved."

I remember watching a television show as a kid, a detective show. They would always begin the plot with, "Ladies and gentlemen, the story you are about to hear is true. The names have been changed to protect the innocent." It is interesting to understand that not one name has been changed from the Gospel writings—not one story and not one name! The Gospel writers do not "protect the innocent" because they know the truth; there are no "innocent" people. Even the disciple Paul would cry out his frustrations with himself: "Oh, what a miserable person I am! Who will free me from this life that is dominated by sin and death?" (Rom. 7:24). And then he continues with those famous words, "So now there is no condemnation for those who belong to Christ Jesus" (Rom. 8:1).

Why do I write this? I write this because the title of this devotional book is *Sincerely Seen*, or "sine cera," and it literally means

Wrapped Up in Sine Cera-ity.

"without wax." Remember how the buyer at the market lifts up the vessel to see it in the light, making sure there are no cracks in it that have been filled with wax? Remember even more that when the vessel is used, if it has wax in the cracks, it will leak sooner or later? It wasn't really a sincere vessel; it was cracked. It couldn't really hold liquids.

Now apply this to the lives of the people in these Gospel stories. Each of the persons recorded in John's Gospel, as well as in the other Gospels, is a vessel with cracks and flaws. Each one came from flawed families; they made flawed choices in their lives. Each of us is *not* without flaw or the fake filling of wax. But John and the other writers of the New Testament write without flaw, without wax-filled stories, so that readers can take comfort! God's Spirit wrote through flawed vessels about the only One who is without wax—Sincere—Christ Jesus—Alive. And now He is interrupting these flawed-vessel lives for the purpose of bringing them love in their rejection, peace in their torments, joy in their sorrows, patience in their trials, goodness in their evil, kindness in their meanness, faithfulness in their relationships, gentleness in their anxiousness, and self-control in their selfishness—the fruit of God's Spirit (Gal.5:22–23).

Do you doubt your own need for Christ?

Here's a little test I do periodically. I go through 1 Cor. 13, which is about the definition of love, and I make a list. I check the items I have failed at just that week—no use in looking over a long period. This is not a practice of self-loathing, which does no good. This is a practice of raising my own vessel-heart up to the light of God's definition of love for the purpose of seeing my need for Christ, for confession, forgiveness, and working toward wholeness in Him.

1Cor.13:1-7: If I speak in the tongues of mortals and of angels, but do not have love, I am a noisy gong or a clanging cymbal. And if I have prophetic powers, and understand all mysteries and all knowledge, and if I have all faith, so as to remove mountains, but do not have love, I am nothing. If I give away all my possessions, and if I hand over my body so that I may boast, but do not have love, I gain nothing. Love is patient; love is kind; love is not envious or boastful or arrogant or rude. It does not insist on its own way; it is not irritable or resentful; it does not rejoice in wrongdoing, but rejoices in the truth. It bears all things, believes all things, hopes all things, endures all things. (*NRSV*)

> Love is:
> Patient
> Kind
> Not envious or boastful or arrogant or rude
> Not irritable or resentful
> Does not rejoice in wrongdoing
> Rejoices in the truth
> Bears all things
> Believes all things
> Hopes all things
> Endures all things

On a good day, I fail at least half of this list. How about you?

What's my purpose in bringing this truth to the front?

The stories John writes are stories about failed people interrupted by Christ Himself, so that He—Jesus—could love them, bring His kingdom to them, and make them whole. In John's stories, he will even write about how Jesus talks about you and me: "I ask not only on behalf of these but also on behalf of those who believe in me through their word, that they may all be one. As you, Father, are in me and I am in you, may they also be in us, so that the world may believe that you have sent me."

And know that you are Sincerely Seen today, at this moment, even in your not-so-sincere ways of life.

How are you experiencing being seen by Jesus today?

Jesus Christ—Sincerely God Alive!

Scene (Seen) 37

Broken and Hidden Matzah

John 20:1–10

Early on the first day of the week, while it was still dark, Mary Magdalene came to the tomb and saw that the stone had been removed from the tomb. So she ran and went to Simon Peter and the other disciple, the one whom Jesus loved, and said to them, "They have taken the Lord out of the tomb, and we do not know where they have laid him." Then Peter and the other disciple set out and went toward the tomb. The two were running together, but the other disciple outran Peter and reached the tomb first. He bent down to look in and saw the linen wrappings lying there, but he did not go in. Then Simon Peter came, following him, and went into the tomb. He saw the linen wrappings lying there, and the cloth that had been on Jesus' head, not lying with the linen wrappings but rolled up in a place by itself. Then the other disciple, who reached the tomb first, also went in, and he saw and believed; for as yet they did not understand the scripture, that he must rise from the dead. Then the disciples returned to their homes. (*NRSV*)

"Each day brings us a deeper experience of our saving God, each day shows us, anew, how deeply men need His salvation, each day reveals the power of the Gospel, each day the Spirit strives with the sons of men; therefore, never pausing, be it ours to tell out the glorious message of free grace" (Spurgeon). Mary Magdalene would bring the "glorious message of free grace!"

I bet you are wondering, after reading three Gospel accounts of the resurrection and having started the fourth, the following two questions: How do all these stories come together? Do they come together?

> All of the people, written about in the four Gospels, claimed to have seen Jesus alive. Mary Magdalene, the other Mary, and the other women, Peter and John, the disciples, the five hundred who witnessed Jesus alive, and the multiple appearances of Jesus alive. Notice there is only one mention—by Paul, the early church apostle of Christ—of Jesus meeting a group of over five hundred people (1 Cor. 15:6). It seems that the writers appreciated Jesus' one-on-one moments with people. Many theologians have studied the progression of events and it seems most have come to conclusion that the stories will not fit together perfectly. This is what makes it more human and more believable. The writers weren't trying to prove anything to anyone. They were just reporting what they knew.

Even though John writes about Mary running back to tell him and Peter, this section is so full of peculiar details. Make a list of the details in this story, and remember, just because "the other Mary" isn't mentioned here, it doesn't mean she wasn't with Mary Magdalene. Don't get caught up in the seemingly different reports of the risen Jesus. Read from the writer's point of view, John the fisherman's perspective. This is John, the beloved disciple; the John who leaned against Jesus during Passover and asked Him who would betray him. This is the John who went with Peter and James to the mountain and saw Jesus transformed; the John whom Jesus asked (along with Peter and James) to come pray with Him in the Garden of Gethsemane.

Make a list of these fishermens'' details:

What is John's comment after they go to the tomb of Jesus? (Hint: verses 9 and 10.)

What choices could John and Peter have made?

Broken and Hidden Matzah

What did they choose to do at the end of all that they saw?

Why do you think they made the choices they made?

What was the result of their choices?

What was going on with Mary and the women during this time?

What do you learn about these people from this story?

What do you learn about God from this?

How do you feel encouraged by this story in your daily life?

I do believe that John is very engaging and completely human in this story! He could have sermonized; he could have hidden many details; but instead, he was honestly human. No wonder he was so endearing to Jesus and others. John writes the details of the race to the tomb: he and Peter were both running fast, but John states (in verse four) that he, John, ran faster. And if you missed the bragging rights of John there, he will write it two more times, in verse six, "And so Simon Peter also *came following him*," and verse eight, "So the other disciple, *who had come first to the tomb*, also entered in and he believed." Notice that John mentioned his athletic ability, which is quite humorous. Also notice what John did in this list of actions:

- Arrived at the tomb first
- Stooped and looked in
- Saw the linen wrappings there
- Did not go in
- Watched Peter run in
- But saw and believed.

Meanwhile, Peters' actions are:

- Ran to the tomb, slower than John
- Ran past John and stooped to enter the tomb first
- Saw the linen wrappings lying there

- Saw the face cloth which had been on Jesus' head, not lying with the linen wrappings but rolled up by itself.

They both would leave the tomb and go back to their homes, John believing—in what? (He does not say.) And Peter—well, there was no comment from him. He is quiet for possibly one of the first times in his life!

Now read this again, only slower. The face cloth was rolled up and separated from the linen wrappings. If the disciples were the ones who stole the body of Jesus, as the guards would report to the people, and if that story were circulated as the reason Jesus' tomb was empty, then why was the face cloth so neatly rolled up? And why were the linen wrappings lying there? Maybe, in their haste to steal the body, the wrappings were just hastily discarded? That would mean the disciples came at night while the guards were sleeping and stole Jesus' naked body from the tomb. In Jewish tradition, it was defiling for a devout Jew to touch a dead body; it was also defiling to do so on a Sabbath, and to touch a naked dead body!

Another question is this: Why in the world would they take the time to roll up the face cloth? I've heard it said that a face cloth was sometimes folded in a special manner to signify the guest's pleasure and desire to return again. In any case, the face cloth being rolled up is a detail that merits thought. I love the folded napkin because it shows the imagination and detailed description of John. Could Jesus have been signaling to His beloved friends that He loved them and wanted to come back? My view is that it was an exclamation that Jesus would not abandon His followers. He would not abandon them because He is God, not because of the disciples' works or their lack of works, their faith or their lack of faith! He is God, and His lack of abandonment was purely based on His own love for His one-on-one friends!

But if you choose to discard this story as a fabrication, you are still left with the fact that the face cloth—the *soudarion* (as it was called in Bible times, when it was a handkerchief used to

Broken and Hidden Matzah

swathe the head of a corpse)—was separated from the linen wrappings (Strong, G4676). The body of Jesus had not been stolen. The "thieves" would not have discarded the linen wrappings when taking the body. They might have discarded the face cloth in their haste, but not the grave clothes. They most certainly would not have taken the time to fold up the face cloth in their fear-driven moments of hijacking Jesus' body from the tomb! Was it twisted into a specific form while the centurion guards lay asleep? And by the way, centurion guards don't sleep on the job, because if they lose the prisoner that they are guarding, they lose their own lives!

There is another detail about this face cloth that was twisted and laying in the tomb. The word for the "face cloth" is the same word used for the napkin that was, and is still, used at the Passover meal. Since the Middle Ages, the Jews would celebrate the Passover meal with three ceremonial matzahs. One of those ceremonial moments would be when a matzah was broken, wrapped in a napkin, and hidden for the children to find at the end of the Seder meal; it was called the *tzafun*, which means "hidden." Whoever found the broken piece would be given a prize, so it was highly valued by the children at the meal. When it was found, the child's father would ransom it with a prize, and then it would be eaten in silence—as a reminder of the brokenness of the matzah and the brokenness of life. Life is still not whole, a particularly for the Hebrew as they do not believe Jesus was the Messiah. It was written:

> But it is toward the Passover of the Future that our memories are directed. *The redemption is not over.* There is fear and poverty and sickness. There is a trembling on earth. Around us are the plagues of pollution, and images of fiery nuclear explosions in the clouds, not like the cloud of glory and the pillar of fire that led our ancestors through the wilderness. The broken matzah speaks to our times, shakes us by the shoulders and shouts into our hearts, "Do not bury your spirit in history. Do not think it is over, complete, that the Messiah has come and you have nothing to do but to wait, to pray, to believe." (Rabbi Harold Schulweis)

Could the grave, that John and Peter were running to look at, represent God's heart to pursue all of His children through the reality of His broken, hidden, tomb-bound body? Could John's details be a bridge of redemption, connecting Passover with the empty tomb? Could John the Baptist have been right in his proclamation: "Behold, the Lamb of God, who takes away the sins of the world," as he pointed to Jesus (John 1:29)? Oh, God's amazing details as the still-unbelieving friends of Jesus began to show up at the tomb like children searching for the *tzafun*, and then discovering the piece of matzah. "While they were eating, Jesus took a loaf of bread, and after blessing it he broke it, gave it to the disciples, and said, 'Take, eat; **this is my body**'" (Matt. 26:26).

John and Peter were men running to the tomb, like the Passover children running to find the broken and hidden piece of matzah. They arrived at the tomb only to find that the "piece," or his body, was no longer there. All that they saw was a face cloth rolled in a special way. There are legends that say that the manner in which the face cloth was folded was a statement used by John to remind people of the tradition that dinner guests, at that time, would occasionally do. They would fold a napkin a special way in order to express their delight of the meal and the desire of wanting to return. I think that the sight of the folded-up face cloth was pointing to the "dinner guest" who was not dead but alive, the Son of God, the Son of Man—Jesus! Jesus called Himself the "bread of life' and literally John and Peter were running to find him like children looking for the "hidden matzah."

Jesus Christ—Son of God, Son of Man

Scene (Seen) 38

Regular, Normal, Everyday Life

John 20:11-13

But Mary stood weeping outside the tomb. As she wept, she bent over to look into the tomb; ¹² and she saw two angels in white, sitting where the body of Jesus had been lying, one at the head and the other at the feet. ¹³ They said to her, "Woman, why are you weeping?" She said to them, "They have taken away my Lord, and I do not know where they have laid him."

Mary Magdalene was a leader of leaders, always ready to move forward, and I believe she was a woman with a larger-than-life picture of Jesus.

What is your picture of Jesus these days?

Does He seem to ignore your prayers?

Is He just a fix-it kind of guy?

Is He seemingly too busy for you?

Are you too busy for Him?

Has He meant anything to you in the past?

What does He mean to you now?

Mary wept as she stooped to look into the tomb. She saw two angels sitting at the grave. The questions are numerous if one thinks through the four Gospel accounts of the resurrection. Did Mary go by herself, or was she with other women? John writes only about Mary. Matthew, Mark, and Luke write about Mary being with other women. What might be happening here? Are these errors in the manuscripts? I don't think so! What if Mary Magdalene couldn't sleep, and went early in the morning to check things out? What if the women went early with Mary Magdalene, and then came back to report it to His disciples? But Mary Magdalene just couldn't do her work, so she returned to the tomb. Or what if she never left the tomb, and the women told the disciples? Matthew says, "They left the tomb quickly," and Jesus showed up to them. What if Jesus had a conversation with Mary Magdalene while the others ran to get the disciples? Mark says, "He first appeared to Mary Magdalene" (Mark 16:9). Maybe she reported to all, but only the women believed and went with her back to the tomb.

It doesn't matter. Remember, these are short reports of Jesus alive, and they were written through the eyes of different people. All the details are not going to be included. John will refer to this in the last verse of John 21, as we will see. What if the other women were with Mary, and John just doesn't write about them? In fact, Luke doesn't mention that any of the women saw Jesus!

And while we try to figure out how this really happened, let's not forget to see the majesty of the events. In the Old Testament, Moses was asked by God to have the children of Israel build a tabernacle that would include the famous Ark of the Covenant, the Holy of Holies. God said that His Glory would rest there as He guided them through the wilderness to Jerusalem. On that Ark of the Covenant was to lie a magnificent top called the Mercy Seat. On that Mercy Seat, which was made of gold, would be two carved golden cherubim facing each other, with their wings facing forward, as if to say to all, "This place is Holy and Sacred."

Now think about it: here at the tomb, close to fifteen hundred years later, Mary Magdalene stands on the precipice of a no longer regular-normal-everyday life. There in the tomb stand two angels, facing each other at this most incredibly merciful place, the Mercy

Regular, Normal, Everyday Life

Seat, where Jesus, the Holy One, defeats death forever and gives mercy to all who will call Him LORD—Yahweh. What if these are amazing details of angels on a mercy seat in the wilderness (the tomb of Jesus), facing each other, and reminding all who approach that Yahweh is the Almighty God, and Holy is His Name? God has gone full circle, not forgetting His people even when they think that all is hopeless and that God has abandoned them!

Mary Magdalene is a single woman who is a strong leader with a zealous love for Jesus. I just don't think she could bring herself to go back to a regular-normal-everyday-life again. Knowing these resurrection stories, the question is whether any of us can ever go back to a regular, normal, everyday life. Can you? Can I? Can any of us, after meeting Jesus personally, alive in the Spirit, whom we will one day see alive in the flesh, ever go back to regular, normal, everyday life?

Maybe this is why the angels were asking Mary Magdalene this very direct question: "Woman, why are you weeping?" I mean, the angels of all creation should know why she is weeping! Jesus, the Christ, the Nazarene, was killed, and is buried in a tomb! Why wouldn't she be crying? Maybe the two women named Mary came back a second time to talk to an angel or two again, sitting at the place where Jesus had lain. Mary, still not really believing, tells them, "We're here because they have taken my Lord, and we do not know where they put him." It would make sense that Mary would say this, since that very morning the news was being spread by the guards that Jesus' body had been stolen by His disciples (Matt. 28:13–15). Even after being told by the angels and going to tell the disciples, and hearing the rumors going around, Mary is telling the angels that someone stole the body; she was desperately weeping and without hope. And the angels were helping her to voice her heart and soul. No more regular, normal, everyday life! Mary got to blurt it out, and what came next would be astounding.

Maybe you have lost hope in humanity at this very moment. Maybe you just don't see an answer to the issues of regular, normal, everyday trials. Maybe you feel invalidated by humanity, or misunderstood! I have felt invalidated and misunderstood, but I have also invalidated and misunderstood others. Crisis is resolved through humility in regular, normal, everyday life, through being able to admit that we don't have the answers, and we don't have our lives fitting together in regular, normal, everyday boxes. WE are desperate for an Alive Savior to come and transform our regular-normal-everyday lives. I want to see into the hearts of people's lives, and to look with compassion. I want to do this because the living Jesus has done this for me. In my classes I have had moments when I unfortunately misunderstood and invalidated people (I am human), and I have found that in every situation, if I stand firm in truth and love, and with humility of heart take a posture of seeking forgiveness and compassion, it has taught others not to be defensive, to be slow to speak and quick to listen. There is no greater joy than to see others through the eyes of Jesus as He has seen me, in my regular, normal, everyday life. When I do this, I find the secret of following Jesus is as St. Francis of Assisi once prayed: "O Divine Master, grant that I may not so much seek to be consoled as to console; to be understood, as to understand; to be loved, as to love; for it is in giving that we receive, it is in pardoning that we are pardoned, and it is in dying that we are born to eternal life."

Jesus Christ—Almighty God, and Holy Is His Name!

Scene (Seen) 39

You Are My All in All

John 20:14–20

When she had said this, she turned around and saw Jesus standing there, but she did not know that it was Jesus. Jesus said to her, "Woman, why are you weeping? Whom are you looking for?" Supposing him to be the gardener, she said to him, "Sir, if you have carried him away, tell me where you have laid him, and I will take him away." Jesus said to her, "Mary!" She turned and said to him in Hebrew, *Rabbouni*, which means "teacher." Jesus said to her, "Do not hold on to me, because I have not yet ascended to the Father. But go to my brothers and say to them, 'I am ascending to my Father and your Father, to my God and your God.'" Mary Magdalene went and announced to the disciples, "I have seen the Lord;" and she told them that he had said these things to her. When it was evening on that day, the first day of the week, and the doors of the house where the disciples had met were locked for fear of the Jews, Jesus came and stood among them and said, "Peace be with you." After he said this, he showed them his hands and his side. Then the disciples rejoiced when they saw the Lord. (*NRSV*)

Have you ever had someone you love die, and a week later you are walking somewhere, and you think you see that person? In that situation it takes you back, so much, in fact, that it rocks your world, and you have to leave, just to go to a grieving place! It is good for us to contemplate what Mary might have been going through. I wonder if Mary Magdalene was beside herself! No, she hadn't thought she had seen her dead friend; she just wanted to find the grave robbers and get the dead body back to the tomb so that she could somehow grieve and anoint the body of her dead friend. She was a true friend, setting out with a mission, and now all of it was coming unglued, unraveled, and undone. Then, as John writes, "She turned around." Dr. Dale Bruner, in his commentary on John, writes these most amazing words:

> "In the one or two seconds this turn took, I imagine the world shifting ever so slightly on its axis, and at about this turn's one-second midpoint trajectory, history, too, moved almost imperceptibly from BC to AD. A second before this turn there is a woman in the deepest human despair in the agonizing presence of unconquerable death; a second after the beginning of this turn there is a woman in the deepest possible human elation—in the presence of the death-conquering Central Figure of history." (Bruner,1155)

We can wonder why Mary didn't recognize Jesus at first (but if you have been in grief, you know just how dull your mind can become, and how little you connect the dots of life). We can wonder why in the world Mary, a woman, is the first to see the Alive Jesus (and I say to that, "Why NOT?"). We can wonder about many details, but in reality, what's most important is that JESUS IS ALIVE! Jesus calls out her name, Mary, which in the original language was Miriam. What music filled the air at the sound of his voice calling her by name? I could only long for the day to hear my loved ones who have passed call out my name, yet I cannot imagine the King of Kings calling out my name, but HE WILL. John records that Mary responds with *Rabbouni*, which is not the formal "teacher" but "MY TEACHER." Mary calls Jesus hers. He is her all in all.

I remember being at a Young Life camp called Malibu, in Canada, and being very tired. We had all spent the day unloading the boat of bags of flour and supplies for a camp of five hundred, and then we met for hours to go over the camp schedule. Then we got on the boat again to go three hours back to the dock to greet the leaders and their campers. After that, we brought them back across the inlet to get them moved in. Finally, we were to run a full evening of festivities and have a Young Life club with a message about Jesus, ALL IN ONE DAY!

Literally, that was nine hours on a boat, crossing the inlet three times, and then a full day's worth of working camp! I crawled into bed at midnight, and then got up early the next morning to begin a full day of camp with events, meetings, and a Young Life club. There were leaders who needed mattresses or had other needs, and I thought, "How in the world am I going to do this for a whole month?" I was walking to dinner that night, making sure the campers were all out of their rooms and in the dining hall, when I heard the workcrew singing in the meeting room above me. The workcrew were high school students who had signed up for a month to volunteer to do the laborious work of serving their peers. What struck me was their heart to serve! These were high school students who didn't know much, except that Jesus is the God they wanted to follow and serve, no matter the difficulty! Here is the song they were singing, which is by Dennis Jernigan:

> You are my strength when I am weak
> You are the treasure that I seek
> You are my all in all
> Seeking You as a precious jewel
> Lord to give up, I'd be a fool
> You are my all in all
> Jesus Lamb of God, worthy is Your name
> Jesus Lamb of God, worthy is Your name
> Taking my sin, my cross, my shame
> Rising again I bless your name
> You are my all in all
> When I fall down You pick me up

When I am dry You fill my cup
You are my all in all
Jesus Lamb of God, worthy is Your name
Jesus Lamb of God…

"You are my all in all." These words struck my soul that night! If high school kids could sing after forty-eight hours of intense labor, why couldn't I? I have tried to accept this workcrew challenge, this divine moment in my life, ever since. I believe Mary Magdalene, at this moment in her life, understood the words of that song: "Taking my sin, my cross, my shame, rising again I bless your name, You are my all in all!" Jesus, You are MY RABBI, My Teacher, MY All in All. As Bruner would write, "So in six short syllables, 'Ma-ri-am' and 'Rab-bou-ni,' and in just about that many seconds, the world became a different place. Death, once final, has met its match. There is a reality—Someone—more final than death. That is the compact meaning of this meeting."

We can wonder again at the reason Jesus would tell Mary Magdalene not to hold on to him. But he gives the reason, and it's not because she was being inappropriate! Naturally, she jumped to hug him; of course she clung to him; of course she was in unexplainable joy; and of course she wanted to hold him tightly. But this was not Jesus' plan. He did not shy from her embrace but met it full on, and then explained it was "because I have not yet ascended to the Father. But go to my brothers and say to them, 'I am ascending to my Father and your Father, to my God and your God.'"

Mary could not keep this news or this Jesus for herself; no one can. Mary, and all of us, are to GO. It is astounding that Jesus would say, "I am ascending to my Father." I don't know what to focus on first! It is like a treasury of golden words. Jesus would ascend to the Father. Did that mean he was going right then? Dr. Bruner believes this is so. Jesus' glorified body gave him full physical access to ascend to the Father, no longer limiting himself, as Paul explained to the Philippians, "who, though he was in the form of God, did not regard equality with God as something to be exploited, but emptied himself, taking the form of a slave, being born in human likeness. And being found in human form, he humbled himself and became obedient to the point of death—even death on a cross" (Phil. 2: 6-8).

Maybe Jesus was back and forth between his friends on earth and his Father in heaven. What is amazing is this statement: "I am ascending to my Father and your Father, to my God and your God." God is no longer His Father and His God; as the second Adam, He has made it possible for God to be *their* Father and *their* God: "my Father and your Father, my God and your God." Just as Mary Magdalene stated it, "My Rabbi," "My Teacher," My All in All.

So, what does this look like for you? What does All in All mean for you?

Who is this Jesus to you? Is He your Rabbi, your all in all?

As Dr. Bruner wrote, "She is the first person privileged to say these words in the Gospel of John. If her announcement is true, then there is, indeed, a Gospel." As the Workcrew sang, it is true: "When I fall down you pick me up; when I am dry You fill my cup; You are my all in all!" Amen and Amen.

Jesus Christ—Our All in All!

Scene (Seen) 40

There You Are _____.

John 20:19

When it was evening on that day, the first day of the week, and the doors of the house where the disciples had met were locked for fear of the Jews, Jesus came and stood among them and said, "Peace be with you." (*NRSV*)

This day just doesn't seem to end. Do you ever have a day like the one Dr. Bruner describes in his commentary?

One is almost moved to ask: how can one calendar day support such cosmic events? But the convex of this concave Resurrection is mission, and, the two have to happen almost exactly together, on the same day, because this Great Miracle requires this Great Mission, immediately and urgently. (Bruner, 1161)

This day was filled with women at the tomb, an earthquake, stones rolled away, soldiers frozen, conversations with angels, Jesus telling the women to go and tell others to go, the followers of Jesus running back and forth between the tomb and Jerusalem, "centurion soldiers meeting with authorities and consulting together," and the high priest gathering a scoop of dirt and a small sample of the barley crop—the spring of hope for the future and the beginning of the celebration that day (for the Jews), the Feast of First Fruits. What symbolism the priest had in his hands! His hands carried the first of fruits from the ground, a promise fulfilled by God. Each year, the Jewish people celebrated this: the brand-new growth and the promise of a harvest. First Fruits was a

There You Are _____.

celebration of the "peeking out" of new life, making the first fruit new out of the death of the seed.

Yes, indeed, it was as Bruner described it: "A day of Great Miracle, a day of Great Mission!" The disciples were afraid, but new hope breaks through their locked doors. Jesus came and stood right in the middle of them, and said, "Peace be yours." Jesus in the middle was in the middle. Jesus was not knocking on those locked doors, but in the middle of the room with his friends. It's messy in the middle. None of us is exempt from the messy middle of life's dance. In our lives, as in a dance unfolding, there is the first call (act), the middle call (act), and the third and final call (act). The middle call can be short or long; it's not up to us. The middle of our life story can be up or down, chaotic or agreeable, dark or light, and definitely full of paradoxes. Then, one day, we will be in our own third and final call, whether known or unknown, and we might have time to look back, come to understanding, and be like Robin Williams in the movie *Hook*.

Williams plays the stressed-out, sellout adult who has forgotten who he really is, Peter Pan. The Lost Boys try to convince him that he needs to fight Captain Hook and save his own children. He flees until the crisis moment when he kneels down, trying to figure out who he really is in life. One of the Lost Boys takes Williams's face in his hands, mushing it and pushing it around his eyes to get rid of the wrinkles of time weathered on his face until finally, after a moment of suspense to all, the boy says, "Oh, there you are Peter."

Williams finally passes from foolishness to acceptance that he is indeed the real Peter Pan. I believe the middle of our life is the place where we come face to face with our identities; the good and the bad. In that middle part of life, we are challenged to give Christ permission to shift through our lives to reveal the things we have buried in the chaos of our earlier years. And by the way, I think the little boy who is pushing back the face of Williams is like Christ). He tells us to stop, to look into his eyes, to surrender our schedules, plans, and dreams into his trial-weathered, nail-scarred hands. When we surrender, we get to move with Him out of our middle and into His will for us, into our true identity. Our true identity is found when Jesus grabs us, whether in an active adventure or the quiet of solitude, and says, "There you are, _____" (put your name in this blank).

Jesus, with a healed yet cross-scarred body, walks through locked doors and into the middle of our living, not with questions like, "Where were you when I needed you?" or "Whatever were you thinking when you made that decision?" Instead, without blaming or shaming us, Jesus says, "Peace be with you." All disciples in that room were in different "middles" in their lives, some questioning, some avoiding. NONE were without failures of some sort. Jesus says to them, "Peace be with you."

And so I ask you, my fellow time travelers, what does the middle of your life look like? Is it tumultuous, quiet, disarrayed, or in order? However it is, you are in the middle, in the messy middle, and you need the Lord of the Dance to come to you and say, "Peace be with you."

Now it's your turn. Write in your journal, or just go for a walk, and think about the middle of your life right now (young or old). Then humble yourself enough to get down on your knees and let Jesus grab your face, pushing back your life's stresses and saying to you, "There you are, _____. Peace be with you."

Jesus Christ—the Lord of Our Dance!

Scene (Seen) 41

Battle Scars to Glory

John 20:19–23

After he said this, he showed them his hands and his side. Then the disciples rejoiced when they saw the Lord. Jesus said to them again, "Peace be with you. As the Father has sent me, so I send you." When he had said this, he breathed on them and said to them, "Receive the Holy Spirit. [23] If you forgive the sins of any, they are forgiven them; if you retain the sins of any, they are retained." (NRSV)

It is human nature to show and talk about our battle scars! I can't tell you how many times my sons and their friends, and my husband and his friends, have boasted about their injuries around the table as my stomach turned and flipped at these gruesome table topics! Why do they have to talk about them while we are eating? I mean, why such detail, and why such drama? And then the pictures on the phones! Please do not send me your injury pictures! Ugh! Is the measure of one's strength scaled to the measure of one's wounds?

And yes, women also gladly boast about their trials in baby deliveries and various other wounds from past adventures. It is human nature to talk about the mishaps of life. There are so many videos of people falling and dangers unknown. What is it in our nature that makes us love to talk about "that time when we hung on a mountain wall for dear life" or "scaled a tree before the onslaught of a wild animal?" The adventures are as varied and numerous as the stars in the heavens; all the sufferings, the near misses, the moments of being saved as well as the dismal life failures—they are abundant. Are these just life experiences that vanish through the days, weeks, and years? Or is there One who dutifully pays attention to each detail, each broken bone and broken heart, and each tear that falls?

> **Do you ever feel "missing?" Do you ever experience the "why am I going through this battle" moment? Does anyone really care? Does it matter in the scope of eternity? Or what about having a "just for today" moment?**

"'Peace be with you!' And when he had said this, he showed them his hands and his side." Jesus walked into a closed-door meeting, uninvited, said "Peace be with you," and then showed his battle scars to all who had passively or aggressively denied him. How does the God of the universe, who created the animals from which the leather straps that came down upon his back were made, who called Simon "Peter" and John "his Beloved," who created the wood on which He was hung—how does this God talk about His battle scars to these people? And why did He do this? Did He show them to shame them? No! Did He show them to boast to them? No!

What if Jesus did this to teach those who would lead how to be vulnerable? What Jewish man would open his robes to show his wounds? I don't think they would, because they were a society of honor and shame. That meant you didn't tell your weaknesses, your failures, or your humiliations in public. Yet here was the Son of God, lifting his robes to show his side, again laying aside his position and humbling himself. He might have been teaching them to share with each other their deepest, darkest scars to help them understand, once and for all, that there's not one battle scar, not one cry, not one tear, not one life-threatening or life-defeating adventure that escapes the eyes of his Father. Then they, in turn, would have strength to teach others this principle.

Nothing escapes the eyes of our Father, and he will bring good out of our scars. Even the apostle Paul would learn this lesson, as he writes to the church in Corinth, 2Corinthians 12:8-9: "Three times I appealed to the Lord about this, that it would leave me, but he said to me, 'My grace is sufficient for you, for power is made perfect in weakness.' So, I will boast all the more gladly of my weaknesses, so that the power of Christ may dwell in me" (*NRSV*).

The mark of a follower of Jesus is trusting the God of REDEMPTION enough to share his or her weaknesses, not in a prideful manner, but in a way that shows people that he or she is being made whole and healed, no matter the cost. God is about healing scars.

Can you imagine the Son of God rolling up His robe to show His beloved brothers the scar over His heart?

It is one thing to show the battle wounds of those nail-driven holes in His hands, but quite another to show His friends the deep wound over His heart! This is what I think John, His beloved disciple, wanted to say in his very human writing, in verse twenty: "And when He had said this, He showed them **both** His hands and His side!" Jesus reminds His friends, first by showing them His carpenter-healing, miracle-working, nail-driven hands; then He bends down and rolls up His robe and reveals His heart wound. Heart wounds matter to Jesus, and heart wounds matter to His Father in heaven!

What did the disciples feel as they saw the healed yet scarred holes in His wrists? The beloved John, with great insight, writes that as Jesus read the faces of His followers—as a pastor reads his congregation, or a shepherd tends his lost sheep—Jesus unflinchingly says, "Peace be with you. As the Father has sent me, so I send you." When he had said this, he breathed on them and said to them, "Receive the Holy Spirit. If you forgive the sins of any, they are forgiven them; if you retain the sins of any, they are retained" (vv. 21–23).

Can you imagine the silence in that room as the disciples stared at Jesus' scars?

Have you ever stood at a grave site not knowing what to say as they lower your friend's loved one, or even your own loved one's body, down into that dark hole? Have you ever experienced the awkwardness that comes after someone has shown you or told you about their scars or the trauma they have just endured? This might be that same silence.

"So," John writes, "Jesus said to them again, 'Peace be with you; as the Father has sent Me, I also send you.'" Jesus speaks peace, forgiveness, and *shalom* into their hearts. Over and over again, He speaks peace. He came back NOT to condemn, but to bring life, and to bring it abundantly, purposefully: LIFE. And that will be the topic of our next devotion: forgiveness.

Jesus always looks ahead but also addresses the feelings, emotions, and thoughts of the present. "Peace be with you…" The first time He spoke peace was when they saw Him in their room, alive. The second time He speaks peace is to minister to them that truth plus love equals grace. Peace. Jesus comes bringing peace. He doesn't overlook the awkward silence; He addresses it. Nothing is missing from Jesus' self-realization: not one scar, not one word. Oh, how I wish I could have been in that room! The only difference is that I would have been like Mary anointing His body with oil before the crucifixion, kneeling at His feet. I pray your hearts will know the deep, penetrating, lift-up-the-robe-and-be-real kind of love of Jesus.

> **Do you feel like God has missed you? Or maybe you feel the awkwardness of not knowing what to say to another who feels missed?**
>
> How have you missed seeing Jesus roll up His robe to show you His heart wound? What do you think when you picture this?
>
> **Look again and behold the battle scars of Glory, and then write out what you are thinking. Dwell on His reality, and Peace be with you.**

Who are you being called by Jesus to be vulnerable with right now in your life? God is faithful.

"'To whom then will you compare me, or who is my equal?' says the Holy One. Lift up your eyes on high and see: Who created these? He who brings out their host and numbers them, calling them all by name; because he is great in strength, mighty in power, not one is missing" (Isa. 40:25–26).

Jesus Christ—God with Glory Scars!

Scene (Seen) 42

Unless Ultimatums

John 20:24–25

> But Thomas (who was called the Twin), one of the twelve, was not with them when Jesus came. So the other disciples told him, "We have seen the Lord." But he said to them, "Unless I see the mark of the nails in his hands, and put my finger in the mark of the nails and my hand in his side, I will not believe." (*NRSV*)

"Unless I see the mark of the nails in his hands, and put my finger in the mark of the nails and my hand to his side, I will not believe." These were Thomas's "unless ultimatums." His name was Didymus in Greek, Thomas in Hebrew. Thomas is remembered for his doubts, not for his questions, courage, or curiosity—and that's just like humanity *at times*. We seem to remember the "bad" moments in others, but rarely the good in them!

In John 11:15, almost at the end of Jesus' life, Thomas exhorts his friends to follow Jesus. He knew Jesus was heading back to Jerusalem, where he was being sought in order to be killed by the authorities—this is Thomas's courage! Then, in John 14:5, when Jesus is walking and talking about being the Way, the Truth, and the Life, Thomas asks Him, "Lord, we do not know where you are going. So how can we know the way there?" This is honest curiosity. But does is Thomas called Thomas the Courageous or Thomas the Curious? No, he gets labeled Thomas the Doubter. Too bad, isn't it? Side note: **don't be so quick to label others, or even yourself!**

All of Thomas's friends were now believing; they had just seen

Jesus, so the first thing they thought of was to tell Thomas, "We have seen the Lord." They do not say, "We have seen Jesus of Nazareth" or "We have seen the prophet or Teacher;" they said, indeed, "We've seen the Lord!" Why "Lord?" Was it not because He had mastered death, making Jesus the ultimate Master, "the Lord?"

Before the disciples, the Jewish people knew God as "my Lord." In Genesis 15, Abraham, the father of the Hebrew nation, comes by faith to God and calls Him "my Lord." This name of God was first mentioned in the Old Testament: *Adonai*, "my Lord." God was telling Abraham, for the fourth time in the earlier chapters of Genesis, that He would give Abraham three promises: land, seed, and blessing. Yet even though this was Abraham's fourth time being promised, and even though God had spared Abraham's nephew and wife from a near-death experience, Abraham still doubted. Abraham still questioned. Why?

Abraham questioned because he is human. All of us are doubters, skeptics, and curious beings. Abraham would question God in Genesis 15:2: "O my Lord God, what will You give me?" And again in Genesis 15:8: "O my Lord God, how may I know that I will possess it?" Abraham asks the what and how questions, just like Thomas will!

In Genesis 15, God's response is profoundly confusing for us in modern civilization. My husband is a hunter, and he is familiar with "quartering an animal" once it is slain. In Genesis 15, God has Abraham cut animals in half to prepare them for the covenant-making (or promise-making) ceremony. You see, back then the Jewish people slaughtered an animal, cut it in half, and then laid the parts opposite each other to make an aisle between them. Then both parties of a promise-keeping would walk between the pieces. This would seal of the promise, like when we sign a contract. How dramatic is that compared to our signing a piece of paper? I wonder if the promises made in yesteryear stood in one's mind and heart a bit more radically?

I ask this because they would cut an animal, splitting it in half and walking between the pieces, as a way of saying, "Be it done unto me"—meaning slaughtered and quartered—"if I do not uphold my part of this promise." And then the other party would follow suit. Now that's one way to make sure you keep your promise!

In this situation with Abraham, though, old Abe fell asleep during the ceremony. I mean, he was over seventy-five years old! He never walked between the pieces of the slain animals. He doesn't stay up for the answer God would give him to his personal "my Lord" questions; he fell asleep!

Yet while he slept, *God* would walk through the pieces. "When the sun had gone down and it was dark, a smoking fire pot and a flaming torch passed between these pieces. On that day the Lord made a covenant with Abram, saying, 'To your descendants I give this land…'" (Gen. 15:17–18).

A smoking oven and a flaming torch. Now, don't get hung up on these items representing God; He will show up in a burning bush one day, and with flaming tongues of fire at Pentecost. Besides, God can use whatever He wants to represent His side of the promise-keeping ritual. After all, John the Baptist would say (about the Messiah), "I baptize you with water for repentance, but one who is more powerful than I is coming after me; I am not worthy to carry his sandals. He will baptize you with the Holy Spirit and fire." God showed up with Abraham and goes through the pieces, and then turns around and goes back through the pieces without Abraham. God makes the deal for both of them. He knew Abraham would fail in his relationship with his Lord, and God took on both parts of this covenant deal.

What is truly amazing is not the animal pieces but the culturally hidden message to Abraham. Perhaps God was saying something like, "Be it done unto Me, my body broken, if I don't fulfill my promise to you, Abraham." And then, as old Abe slept away his part of the covenant promise, God sealed the deal and finished the covenant promise, with the hidden message that probably went something like this: "And be it done unto Me if you, Abraham, don't fulfill your part of the bargain."

And guess what? Abraham didn't, Jacob didn't, Moses didn't, Joseph didn't, King David didn't, and Peter, John and James didn't. No, none of us fulfill our part of the bargain of holiness in a selfless relationship with "my Lord." This is so outrageous. But for God, we would all forever be doomed to selfishness, unrighteousness, and a broken relationship with God! God upholds *both* parts of the covenant promise because He knew Abraham would not, and neither would we. He never abandons Abraham, and He never abandons us. God takes both parts of the covenant seriously and He fulfilled this covenant once for all with Jesus on the cross.

Jesus took the promise all the way to the cross. He opened up his arms and allowed others to crucify his body, all to hold true to His great promise. God's Son paid *our* part of the covenant promise. We were in a broken relationship with God, so God paid the price of our brokenness: death and separation from the God we chose to be broken from in our lives. He is a promise-keeping, "my Lord" kind of God for Abraham, Thomas, you and me. The promise of a heaven on earth was fulfilled. The promise of land, seed, and blessings unto all the nations, made complete one day as written in the words of Revelation, which were later written by John the Beloved. Jesus couldn't wait to show His promise come true for Thomas the Curious, Thomas the Courageous, Thomas the Twin.

So—when Thomas is told by his friends that they had seen the Lord, is it any surprise that Thomas doubts and exercises great skepticism? Is it any wonder that when we doubt, when we are skeptical and question, that Jesus stands patiently, helping us to see, come, touch, and believe? Now we can't touch, at least not just yet, but we can read God's Word, and He is faithful to present Himself to us. He will show us much about His love poured out, His understandings of our questions, and his strong love, neither forsaking nor abandoning. This is the same love that caused God to pass through those animal pieces *both ways* with Abraham, and commit to be his Lord; it is the same love that God has to commit to Thomas, to you, and to me. Thomas said "unless," and Jesus showed up in spite of Thomas's curiosity, doubts, and obnoxious intellect. Thomas had "unless" ultimatums, and Jesus Christ didn't stomp away, but instead patiently showed Thomas the truth. He is alive.

What are your "unless ultimatums"? No judgment here, I have plenty of my own lessons!

Unless my family member is healed…
Unless I am given…
Unless You show me Your hands and Your side…

What would it mean to call your God "my Lord"?

Whatever your "unless" ultimatums are, be certain: God knows, and God shows to all who seek Him. So then, take some time to think about this. Who is Jesus to you? And don't be surprised if you end up saying, "My Lord and my God."

And by the way, the name Lord is mentioned four times in just this one part of John 20. This kind of faith would have been labeled by Dr. Bruner, appropriately, as "Magdalenic faith" (Bruner, 1140). Thomas's faith is compared with Mary Magdalene's faith—strong and courageous! No matter the name, it's everything for me to say "my Lord." Amen and Amen!

Jesus Christ—My Lord and My God!

Scene (Seen) 43

A Scene to Be SEEN

John 20:26–29

A week later his disciples were again in the house, and Thomas was with them. Although the doors were shut, Jesus came and stood among them and said, "Peace be with you." Then he said to Thomas, "Put your finger here and see my hands. Reach out your hand and put it in my side. Do not doubt but believe." Thomas answered him, "My Lord and my God!" Jesus said to him, "Have you believed because you have seen me? Blessed are those who have not seen and yet have come to believe." (*NRSV*)

How many times does Jesus have to tell me "Peace be with you" for me to know and have peace? How many times does Jesus have to say to me, "And do not be unbelieving but believing?" As many times as it will take, He will tell me "Peace be with you" and "Do not be unbelieving but believing!" And for that reason alone, God is good!

I have seen the Lord raise up winds across bleachers full of kids listening as I spoke to them about the story of Jesus in a boat on a stormy Galilee Sea. Right at the moment when I told them how Jesus calmed the winds and the waves, the winds going across all of us stopped too. My mother asked me how to know Jesus when my father was in the hospital, and I told her my story and shared with her the love of Jesus dying on a cross and rising on that infamous Sunday. Then, as she struggled through the night, I prayed for her all night, only to hear her story in the morning, as she said with a smile on her face, "I know Jesus now."

I have asked the Lord to show me the truth of my own story, and then I had to go help my mother as she battled cancer. Then my uncle asked me out of the blue, "Did your dad abuse you?" I prayed in the Name of Jesus for my father to stop as he came with anger and cursing to attack me as I was helping my mother. And then I watched him stop cold in his tracks and leave the room. I have asked for strength to serve, and then I was given the privilege to sit with my mother at 3:00 a.m. as she breathed her last breath. I literally saw her spirit leave her body as she passed from this world. I have prayed for my father, to ask for forgiveness, and to meet the Lord face-to-face and know love for the first time, only to find out that at the very moment when I was praying for him (120 miles away and unknown to me), he died in his living room. It may have been that he had time with his God to receive the Lord's truth and love; that is in the Lord's mighty hands.

I once officiated at a funeral only to have a man stand up and start walking to the front. Very clearly, he was disturbed, and so, as I calmly talked about Jesus raising Lazarus from the grave, the man stopped and turned around at the Name of Jesus. I have seen a boy flailing on the ground at camp because demonic spirits were trying to keep him from being free. As we held that boy so that he wouldn't hurt himself, we prayed in the Name of Jesus, and the boy was healed! I have seen my own son miraculously healed of a broken bone. I have found my way through darkness and danger. I have asked the Lord Jesus to multiply food when we were feeding kids at our home, only to find out that fifty more kids had joined the party, and God supplied it! I have lived through earthquakes and asked God to get us to the mission place as our car was breaking down. With its engine sputtering, it stopped right in front of the building in Cuernavaca, Mexico, that we needed to get to—and then the car wouldn't start again.

I have watched hundreds of teenagers who had hard hearts give their broken lives to the Lord Jesus. And I have seen teary

A Scene to Be SEEN

faces changed to joy and peace as they received God's love. I have been backpacking with kids in a whiteout, when the guides pulled out the compass only to have it crumble it their hands. The pressure of getting off the top of the mountain was rising, and we gathered to pray because it was our last resort. (Why it was not our first resort I have wondered ever since.) But right then the clouds separated and the guides recognized our mountain location and what to do next—all right after the amen! Miracles and signs are all around, yet I, like Thomas, still have my doubting, my curious questioning, and my anxious times.

All of this and more—not just for Thomas, not just for myself, and not just for all of us. Yet Jesus still says to us, "Peace be with you. Be not unbelieving, but believe." Oh, how I love to see the peace of Christ rest upon faces and hear the words of true confession from young ones who come to Jesus! There is no better place! When people ask me how I keep doing what I am doing, I ask them, "How could I not?" There's an old song by Will Reagan that says it right: "No place I would rather be, there's no place I would rather be, than here in Your love, here in Your love."

I know what Thomas knew that very moment—peace in belief—when he called Jesus "my Lord and my God." He had it right: Jesus is Lord; Jesus is God with us. "Peace," in the Hebrew of the Old Testament, meant "to be complete, to finish, to make whole or restore" (Strong, H7999). I wonder if Jesus was wanting their belief in Him to be complete, and so He was saying "Peace?" The word is *shalem,* and is even used in regard to Solomon completing the building of the Temple (2 Chron. 5:1). God's peace and God's completion is the "no place I would rather be" place.

"Have you believed because you have seen me? Blessed are those who have not seen and yet have come to believe" (John 20:28). Jesus is calling us! You know, He's talking about the ones who believe without having seen. He calls us "blessed." I wonder why? I wonder what the disciples were thinking when He said, "Those who have not seen?" What mysteries Jesus has for all of us, including the ones who stand right there in front of Him. For sure, they were different from that day on.

"From that day on," those of us who believe without seeing have been blessed. And FOR SURE, we may not see, but WE ARE SEEN. That's the very reason I began writing this devotional. I AM SEEN, YOU ARE SEEN, HIS DISCIPLES WERE SEEN, AND THOSE WHOM WE TELL (AND THEY TELL, AND THEY TELL) WILL BE SEEN. These might be resurrection scenes of Jesus and His friends, but most definitely they are more than just scenes for us; these Gospel stories of Jesus' resurrection are LIVING PROOF that Jesus was SEEN and **we** are SEEN!

> Take the time to write out the miracles in your stories and all that you have seen, and all you have learned to trust Jesus for in your life. It's amazing medicine for a waiting and weary heart. The angels in Luke would command the women at the tomb to "Remember," and so must we.
>
> My Miracles, in the Name of Jesus:
>
>
>
>
>
> And then, once you are finished—*shalem*—say out loud to yourself the words Jesus said to Thomas on that day:
>
> "Peace be with you…Do not be unbelieving but believing."

Jesus Christ—God of Peace!

Scene (Seen) 44

Transformation to Melody Halls

John 20:30–31

Now Jesus did many other signs in the presence of his disciples, which are not written in this book. But these are written so that you may come to believe that Jesus is the Messiah, the Son of God, and that through believing you may have life in his name. (*NRSV*)

"These are written so that you may believe…" The essence of this incredible adventure, recorded by this friend of Jesus, is that you and I too may believe! So then, what does John want us to believe?

- That Jesus is the Christ (the Messiah)
- That Jesus is the Son of God

Messiah means Christ or Anointed One. He is the One whom Abraham, Isaac, Jacob, and others, all the way to King David and beyond, were looking for in the birth of each and every Jewish male.

Reading through all these stories, the question still remains: **Who is Jesus?**

If Jesus was only a good friend who died and His friends wanted His name to live on into eternity, so they stole His body and spread a rumor that Jesus rose from the dead, then why in the world would all those friends of Jesus give up their homes, families, and lives to be persecuted (all but one of the eleven disciples were martyred)? And even greater is the question: Why would they sing through their persecutions? Why would their lives be transformed into "halls of melody?"

Why do I call them "halls of melody?" The disciples, as well as all of the friends of Jesus—male and female—had their lives of fear, confusion, trembling, and hiding transformed into "melody" vessels that rejoiced in singing, filled with the story of Jesus Christ and His death and resurrection for all people, for all nations around them! I don't know if you have ever known the fate of the disciples, but rumor has it that:

- Matthew was killed in Ethiopia by sword.
- Bartholomew (Nathaniel) was flogged to death in Asia.
- Andrew was killed on an X-shaped cross in Greece, saying, "I have long desired and expected this happy hour."
- Thomas was killed with a spear while establishing a church in India.
- Matthias (who took the place of Judas Iscariot) was stoned to death, and if that wasn't enough, he was also beheaded.
- Philip traveled to Heliopolis, where he was put in prison and crucified.
- James, a.k.a. James the Less, was beaten, stoned, and clubbed in the head in Jerusalem.
- Thaddaeus, a.k.a. Jude, was crucified in Edessa; some say he was shot with arrows.
- Simon the Canaanite, the Zealot, preached in Africa, then traveled to England and was crucified.
- Peter was killed in Rome by being crucified upside down.
- James, the brother of Jesus, was stoned to death in Jerusalem; this is recorded in Acts 12:3.
- John, the beloved disciple, after supposedly being boiled in oil in Rome and banished to Patmos Island for many years, finally returned to Ephesus and died of old age.

Transformation to Melody Halls

Now, granted, these are traditions taken from Jewish, Roman, or Greek historians; nevertheless, they are truly amazing.

Why in the world would they die for a lie they spread? Many poor souls have died for someone else's lie, but in this case, how would each of these twelve, with different personalities, different careers, different cultural groups, and different calls, proclaim that Jesus is God's Son, the Messiah, the long-awaited Savior, the anointed One, at the risk of their lives? They were all to die, individually, in different countries and at different times. They would all proudly sing or speak, "Jesus is Christ," more proudly as they became transformed souls, or what I would call "melody halls!"

Could it be that they died for the truth, and to pass on this truth to you and me?

Each one was transformed from being fearfully quiet and hiding to being men who couldn't have a hall big enough to share their song of who this Jesus was to them. They were each changed from the inside out, as Jesus would change each person who came into contact with Him. Each one lived and died to tell the good news that Jesus is the Christ, the Son of God.

What does transformed look like? Well, there is one way I can describe it, but it is humorous, and you will have to indulge me. I can understand transformation by remembering an old college prank that I completed. I was a freshman in a dorm called Melody Hall. The reason for the name was that it was a one-story dorm with extremely wide halls that caused everything to echo—a sound-chamber of sorts. Our rooms faced out onto a park, and we were spoiled by large picture windows that overlooked it. My roommate and I had been pranked by our neighbors, so we decided to wait for the perfect opportunity to carry out our retaliatory prank.

The day came when we were ready to proceed, and so we waited until our neighbors had left for class one early morning. Then we called our friends over, and in forty-five minutes we proceeded to unlock our neighbor's room, transport all of its contents—furniture, clothes, books, and dorm-room paraphernalia—out into the park directly across from their window. We placed their beds, stuffed animals, desks, lamps, books, and junk exactly as they had been inside their room! Their room was exactly as they had left it that morning—only OUTSIDE in the park! Then we closed the door to their room and waited. People would walk by the park (of course we guarded their belongings), take a double glance, and then break into laughter as they realized what was happening. The great news of this radical transformation passed throughout the entire university campus, and this was WAY BEFORE CELL PHONES! People came by and took pictures with their cameras, and we all waited for our roommates to return from their classes. It was the perfect set-up because they didn't pass the park to enter the dorm; they had to enter through the front door.

Then the moment came when our beloved suite mates in dear Melody Hall unlocked their door and saw that everything they owned had been removed! They were frozen by the sight of nothing in their room, all of it having been "transformed" in the park outside! Laugher rang throughout Melody Hall that day, and we declared ourselves "even;" vindication ensued, and the news was out: the transformation of Melody Hall! Obviously, we helped them move it all back in and became even closer in the process, if you were wondering about the preposterous idea of revenge!

What have been the inside-out moments of your life?

The lives of these forever friends in the Gospel of John were forever transformed. Transformed into "Melody Halls," singing of the risen Jesus, no longer dead but alive. And not only alive but bringing the good news of life everlasting, of bodies to be transformed the day Jesus comes back. They lived their lives; they told their news; they praised their living God; and they believed in Jesus as the Christ, the Son of God. Their lives were radically transformed. What would life in His name mean? It would mean a life not without suffering but with deep meaning, a life not without loneliness but with profound joy, a life not without struggle, trial, or hardship but with explosive hope and the power of fulfillment, a life not without temptation or fallen moments but one in Christ, the Son of the living God. These life trials are not the end, but they lead us to understand our Lord's heart for us as we read about His love, poured out for us through the trials of the cross. These trials take on a beauty of transformation because God promises us that they are not the final ending. The final ending will be joy in resurrection glory, as this real and true story is recorded in John.

As Dr. Bruner writes in the *Gospel of John Commentary*, "The overwhelming fact, of course, is that the dead Jesus is now alive—that what all these disciples have been experiencing and all that we have been reading is true. Again, can we imagine the "rush," the thrill, the joy—the ecstasy—at this world-changing encounter of the first disciples with the Risen Jesus Christ?"

Bruner would later quote the Yale Church historian Jaroslav Pelikan: "If the Resurrection of Jesus actually happens, then nothing else really matters. If the Resurrection of Jesus did not actually happen, then nothing else really matters" (Bruner, 1163).

I would certainly add that there is no transformation as profound as the transformation of the human soul! Not a Melody Hall, not a caterpillar into a butterfly—nothing is as profound as the New BIRTH of a soul.

What matters to you as you reread these sacredly profound words?

"Jesus performed many other signs in the presence of his disciples, which are not recorded in this book. But these are written that you may believe that Jesus is the Messiah, the Son of God, and that by believing you may have life in his name." (*NRSV*)

Jesus Christ—Transforming God!

Scene (Seen) 45

The Good Ole Days!

John 21:1–4

> After these things Jesus showed himself again to the disciples by the Sea of Tiberias; and he showed himself in this way. Gathered there together were Simon Peter, Thomas called the Twin, Nathanael of Cana in Galilee, the sons of Zebedee, and two others of his disciples. Simon Peter said to them, "I am going fishing." They said to him, "We will go with you." They went out and got into the boat, but that night they caught nothing. Just after daybreak, Jesus stood on the beach, but the disciples did not know that it was Jesus. (*NSRV*)

The phrase "Jesus showed Himself" appears twice in these three verses. I wonder why. It seems to me that when something in Scripture is repeated, it is there for a reason, positioned strategically by the author. What if John was getting ready to tell a story about all of them trying to escape from the drama of the last few days? This is a story of adventure, friendship, stress-relief, and plans interrupted by the very One who had flipped death to life and was clearly changing the routines of the disciples' lives—the risen Jesus!

Peter was exhausted by all these uncontrollable events, for in the past three days he had found himself face-to-face with his own deepest and darkest weaknesses: his betrayal of Jesus in the courtyard at that charcoal fire, in front of a slave girl and others. He was probably remembering the torture happening to his Rabbi, and ultimately, Jesus' demise—the crucifixion. The One called Son of God was killed. But then came the abrupt report of Jesus being seen alive, risen from the dead, and that outrageous event: Jesus revealing Himself to this denier, Peter, and to his friends in the room! This truly was a drama of world-pandemic size. And now it would seem that Peter wanted to run away and find some sort of peace, some sort of normalcy in life, where he could be in control of his own life and rest. It would seem like all Peter wanted to do was something "everyday" again, something he didn't have to put his mind or emotions into, like fishing on his boat. John writes that Simon Peter simply told Thomas, Nathaniel, John, James, and two others who remained nameless, "I'm going fishing."

We all have had THAT moment in time when the stresses and emotions of an outrageously crazy and monumental weekend have happened and all we want to do is something "normal." Right? You might want to take a walk, work out, call a friend and hang out, play video games, plant a garden, or kick a ball. You might want to just chill out and watch a movie with popcorn and your dog or curl up in a chair and read (or fall asleep). Whatever it is, it is brainless, and it requires only your close friends and an occasional word spoken, or better yet, maybe just a nod.

For Peter, it was fishing. He grew up fishing, and to him, there had to be no calmer place, no place more in his control, where he felt at home. These were the only words written, as if John felt the burden as well, for he mentions that they all said, "We'll come with you." They were great friends. They went out that night. It was a calm, quiet night, and dull, with no action. After the charcoal-fire betrayal, it was exactly what Peter wanted: a place devoid of all emotion, a boat on the Galilee Sea where he and his buddies could just do what they had always done before they met Jesus—fishing.

> Do you ever just want to go back to "those simple days?" You know, the good ole days when life was not filled with stress, worry, or trials? Explain those days out loud or write them down.
>
> What was your simple day like? Where did you go? What did you do?

I think we understand Peter. He just couldn't take it anymore. John was with Peter in the boat, and he finishes writing about that night with these surprising words: "And that night they caught nothing." I wonder if they were relieved. Or were they upset that they had caught nothing? Maybe in the eyes of these seven men, it didn't matter that they didn't catch anything. It was as if John were writing how they were feeling: no more emotion, no more grief, no more shock, no more breath taken away, no more fear or surprises, and no more work cleaning the fish! He is writing to his readers, communicating a sense of being still—as still as the waters that seemed to hold no fish. **Let's take a moment to be quiet and think about this picture of our friends on that boat.**

But even in that moment, Jesus would reveal Himself, *for Jesus will never leave us alone* for long! This might be why John writes twice in the first sentence about this fishing adventure, "After these things Jesus *showed himself* again to the disciples by the Sea of Tiberias; and *he showed himself* in this way" (John 21:1). These words ring out with clarity: Jesus will not abandon us, even when we want to just "go fishing!" The word "showed" is *phanero*—"to make visible or known what has been hidden or unknown (whether by words, or deeds, or in any other way; make actual and visible, realized" (Strong, G5319). Was John beginning the story with *phanero* on purpose? Is the main point that Jesus revealed Himself? **Is this all that really matters, the Son of God, the Son of Man, showing Himself?**

As I close this, I see a man walking by a fountain in a park on a glorious spring day, and he is talking on the phone—FaceTime. He seems to be talking with his family. He shows them the fountain and the spring that dresses the trees, and I can tell he just wants them to enjoy the beauty of this day with him. He wants to be near them, and he wants them to be near him.

Isn't that the way of our hearts? The way of our hearts is to be near one another—even when we have had enough! I wonder if Jesus, the Author and Creator of life, wanted to enjoy the lake's beauty with His friends?

The Good Ole Days!

And so—these words carved into the manuscript by John, Jesus' beloved disciple, mean so much. These words might mean not only that the disciples needed rest but that Jesus just wanted to enjoy the moment, enjoy the morning, enjoy the beauty of that sea-spray day, and to reconnect with his beloved friends. Jesus yelled across the water to them. These are beautifully crafted words, simple and true: "Jesus stood on the beach" (John 21:5). Jesus was always wanting to show Himself to His friends. Peter didn't need the "good ole days" of life before his betrayal when he had Jesus calling out to him and his buddies that bright morning, that very day! I wonder if John loved that day? It would be a day for Peter to remember, that's for sure! But that's a different story.

> How has Jesus shown Himself to you in the last twenty-four hours?
>
> What about this story of Jesus is intriguing to you?
>
> How would you see Peter in this story?
>
> How would you see John in this story?
>
> As you reflect on Jesus, the Son of God, the Son of Man, revealing Himself to you, what astounds you about this entire truth? What might you and I have taken for granted in these last few days, weeks, or months?
>
> Now read this part of Psalm 8 and tremble with joy and awe:
>
> "When I consider Your heavens, the work of Your fingers, the moon and the stars, which You have ordained; what is man that you take thought of him, and the son of man that You care for him? Yet You have made him a little lower than God, and You crown him with glory and majesty...O LORD, our Lord, how majestic is Your name in all the earth!" (*NRSV*).

Jesus Christ—the God Who Shows Up!

Scene (Seen) 46

Silence to Frenzy, Nothing to Greatness

John 21:4–8

Just after daybreak, Jesus stood on the beach; but the disciples did not know that it was Jesus. Jesus said to them, "Children, you have no fish, have you?" They answered him, "No." He said to them, "Cast the net to the right side of the boat, and you will find some." So they cast it, and now they were not able to haul it in because there were so many fish. That disciple whom Jesus loved said to Peter, "It is the Lord!" When Simon Peter heard that it was the Lord, he put on some clothes, for he was naked, and jumped into the sea. But the other disciples came in the boat, dragging the net full of fish, for they were not far from the land, only about a hundred yards off. (*NRSV*)

Can you imagine a night spent floating near the shore of a lake with your friends in a boat? You've fished all night and not caught a thing. For any fisherman, not catching a fish can be at least aggravating. But if that fisherman had been through a weekend of failure, suffering, the death of a friend, and outrageous news that the friend, whom you loved and betrayed, was not dead but alive—this would be a startling reality! And then to see that friend on the beach asking you if you had caught anything—that would rock any fisherman's boat!

As Peter and his friends floated on this great sea of Galilee, otherwise known as the Sea of Tiberius, they would be listening to the lapping of the calm waters against the boat. They might have drifted off to sleep now and then, soothed by the familiarity of the waters and the boat; after all, they were fishermen. I imagine the sun would have begun to rise with the yellow, smoky-gray dawn before the colors of day were made vivid—the dawn of another day, and not one fish in their nets. Maybe they didn't ever fall asleep. Maybe it was James who rolled over and opened his eyes to see his friends stirring in the boat, or maybe it was John—no matter; they were all awake. And now hunger and the chill of the early morning air made it clear to them: it was time to bring up the nets and go home. We have all had that moment in the morning, the first glances and the first stomach grumblings—it's time for breakfast!

They were pulling in their nets in the boat, fully aware that they had caught nothing. The word for nothing in the Greek is *oudas*, or "nada, nada, empanada" (as I learned it in Spanish). "Not one thing" is what John remembers. You can almost sense the frustration of a fisherman as he would record it definitively: "They caught nothing." It's such a dichotomy—they would catch nothing in the boat, and then, when Jesus told them to look on the other side, they would catch everything. I wonder if John realized later, as he was writing this story, that with Jesus, their nets in life would always be full of adventures and fishing for people to know Jesus?

The word "nothing" could be considered a "deep-well word"—a word full of impact and significance or a word full of emptiness—isn't that ironic? Those nets might have been a graphic reminder to John, through his later years of serving others, sharing the good news that Jesus was alive, and writing Jesus' words, of just how short all of us come up in life. Life is NOTHING without Jesus. But with Jesus, we have EVERYTHING! What a picture for John to hold onto when he was banished to Cyprus in his later years, after being tortured, and knowing that all of his fellow fishermen were to die martyr deaths. It really would be a difficult reminder if it were not for the fact that JESUS IS ALIVE—and for what would happen next on that Galilean beach.

Have you ever experienced a moment of "nothing?" Take some time to recollect those moments; although difficult to remember, these memories will remind you just how far you have come and how Jesus has carried you.

My moment would be when I came to the reality that all those nightmares of myself as a child were real, and I was left with the "nothing" of a hope that life as a child really wasn't full of love or goodness. It wasn't all bad, but life had its "nothing" moments and I had wanted to block out those "nothing" moments! It's as if the puzzle of my life came together in front of my eyes, and I kept wanting to scatter the pieces in front of me and yell, "That's not really true!"

Don't worry, my friend, for "nothing" moments make space for a view of God beyond all that we could dream or imagine!

Nothing moments in my life bring out the learning opportunities in my life!

Nothing moments in my life clarify to me the Everything that God is!

And so, as these dear fishermen were hauling up those nets, heavy with water but with a "nothingness" of fish, an unrecognizable man on the beach yelled out to them across the waters, about one hundred yards away. "Children, you do not have fish to eat, do you?"

First off, how dare some stranger call those fishermen "children!" What a crazy description of those crusty old fishermen who had spent a night on a boat. It would be outlandish but for one thing—that stranger knew them! If you know anything, you never drill into the hearts of fishermen with "nothing" in their nets after they have been fishing all night! No wonder their answer was a flat "no." Two negatives were mentioned in that moment in time: "nothing" and "no." It's as if they had to admit that they had nothing left in their pockets, their nets, or their hearts. I sure wouldn't have wanted to be on that boat to hear the mumbling, and maybe even the cursing, or at least the question, "Who does that guy think he is?"

It is so ironic to get to the point in life when we have nothing

Silence to Frenzy, Nothing to Greatness

left to give, no strength to try or fix or even argue: "no" is their final answer! John writes that the man on the shoreline responded, "Cast the net to the right side of the boat, and you will find some." Here it is: the teachable moment! They could choose to listen and do the casting or tell him to "shove off!" Charles Spurgeon wrote it accurately in a sermon about the love of God: "Well may each of us who has been for years a student at the Master's feet exclaim, 'I find myself a learner yet.'"

Dr. Bruner had a great insight in his *Gospel of John Commentary*: that this encounter was truly the first "fireside chat," with four essential remarks: "How are you doing? I've got an idea: cast your net starboard. [Then] I'd like to use what you have. Let's have a meal together" (Bruner).

First the question Jesus asked them, then the command: put your nets on the other side. After that, bring what you caught. Finally, let's eat together. If I were they, I would have said "shut up," and I would have gone to another beach far away from that guy! But not these fishermen! They were teachable!

"So they cast their net starboard, and now they were not able to haul the net in because there were so many fish." After this catch, there must have been a silent pause. I have often wondered what the glances among the fishermen were like as they dropped the nets starboard. Were there arguments, or were they all united with an "aye aye, mate" before the awkward but curious silence that fell as they peered over the boat's edge into the depths of the sea? Finally, there must have been an unbelievably bewildering bedlam of joy! The great, deep of the sea of Galilee swirled a superabundance of fish into the net of these seven startled sailors. They couldn't even haul the net aboard because of the greatness of the catch. It is then that John, the writer, makes a profound remark: "It's the Lord!" Just when there is a "nothing" and a "no," there's an "It's the Lord!" **God shows up!**

Peter then threw on his outer garment, maybe a shirt worn by fishermen when they worked, and dove into the waters, being the dramatic man he was, and the rest of the guys were left to haul in the nets and row ashore. Can you imagine the boat: fish jumping, the men eager to get to shore, with the déjà vu of a moment when this had happened before, maybe three years earlier, swimming through the minds of John, Nathaniel, and the rest of the guys?

> When he had finished speaking, he said to Simon, "Put out into the deep water and let down your nets for a catch." Simon answered, "Master, we have worked all night long but have caught nothing. Yet if you say so, I will let down the nets." When they had done this, they caught so many fish that their nets were beginning to burst. So they signaled their partners in the other boat to come and help them. And they came and filled both boats, so that they began to sink. (Luke 5:4–9, *NRSV*)

This was now the mood of that moment: from silence to frenzy, from nothingness to abundance. The nets were full, and life was flipped around, turned upside down, or better, inside out.

> **So—how would you describe your life right now? Silence or frenzy, nothingness or abundance?**

> **Are you in the hard place of "nothing" or "no?"**

> **How does this story encourage you mentally, spiritually, or emotionally?**

> **What do you think it will take for you to see Jesus on the beach of your everyday life and to hear Him calling you "child?"**

> **It was most endearing for Jesus to call them "children" after they caught the fish and knew it was Jesus. Sometimes in life we may not have caught the fish yet, but He stills calls us His children. This is TRUTH.**

> **Take some time to listen, be refreshed, and become teachable to understand that Jesus does have a plan for you, His child. And then look to the morning breaking loose with newness. Listen.**

Jesus Christ—Everything God!

Scene (Seen) 47

Sincerely Seen by a Charcoal Fire

John 21:9–11

> When they had gone ashore, they saw a charcoal fire there, with fish on it, and bread. Jesus said to them, "Bring some of the fish that you have just caught." So Simon Peter went aboard and hauled the net ashore, full of large fish, a hundred fifty-three of them; and though there were so many, the net was not torn. (*NRSV*)

A "charcoal fire" is the phrase the Gospel writer chooses. The only other time a "charcoal fire" is mentioned in Scripture is when John wrote about in John 18:17–18:

> The woman said to Peter, "You are not also one of this man's disciples, are you?" He said, "I am not." Now the slaves and the police had made a charcoal fire because it was cold, and they were standing around it and warming themselves. Peter also was standing with them and warming himself.

The word for charcoal fire is *anthrakia*, which means a heap of "burning coals" (Strong, G439). This would end up being a "full circle" moment in Peter's life.

When we left the story, Peter had jumped into the water, and the rest of the six were rowing back to shore with a net bursting at the seams with fish. Peter jumped from the boat into the water when he heard John say, "It's the Lord." **Would you have jumped in the** water?** I might have if it was really hot. But what I certainly WOULD NOT have done was put on more clothes and then jump in!

I remember being at a Young Life camp in Saranac, New York. On the first night of camp, we always had water games with all the high schoolers and their leaders. We had to take a swimming test to participate; we had to jump into the lake, which, by the way, had the tropical temperature of forty degrees because it was the end of May and the ice had just melted off of Saranac Lake! We had to get into wet suits that were laid out for us, so I grabbed one to put on, as did everyone else. I went over to the side to put it on, as I was older and really felt a bit conscious of my age. I put it on and then walked up to all of my high school friends, saying, "There, ready to go."

They all started laughing and said, "Kathy, you have the suit on backward; the zipper goes in the back." Right then, the lifeguard with the marine-like voice blew his whistle and said, "Okay, jump in," and so I just jumped into that icy lake. The dock was about fifty yards away, and we had to swim to the dock and back. I started out great, but a few strokes into swimming and I felt the zipper, because I had it on backwards, cutting off my capacity to breathe. I honestly thought I was going to go down! I finally got to the dock, and the sweet lifeguard got down on her knees and said, "Are you okay?" With great pride, I breathlessly said, "Yeah," and then just held onto the dock. She lifted me up out of the water, to my embarrassment, and then noticed my wetsuit was on backward and started to talk, stifling laughter. "No wonder! No one can swim with the zipper up in their mouth."

She asked me if I wanted to switch it, and I said no, then jumped into the water. With my old-lady strength and fortitude, I got close to the beach and just sat there in that cold water until I could get out. Everyone was playing volleyball by then and not even looking my way; it's so good to be old! NOT!

That story, my friends, is the nearest I can get to how Peter might have felt as he jumped into the waters with his clothes on. Peter jumped from the boat and swam about one hundred yards in his

Sincerely Seen by a Charcoal Fire

robes to the shore. Drenching, dripping, and dragging, Peter pulled himself out of the waters and, standing on the beach, blinking the Galilee Sea out of his eyes, he looked and saw "a charcoal fire."

> Have you ever had a moment in life when all time seemed to stand still, and your heart beat was arhythmic, and you knew you had been at that same moment in time before? Some call it déjà vu, an "already seen" moment.

Remember the title of this book is *Sincerely Seen*. Why have I decided to call it this? *Sincerely Seen* is the title because either Jesus was "sincerely seen" time after time by His friends or this is some made-up story that they paid the guards off to say, and Jesus really wasn't seen at all. AND if Jesus is seen sincerely, then His friends were being "Sincerely Seen" too. There are no in-betweens! Either Jesus really is God and Sincerely Sees His friends and us, including Peter's betrayals, ours, and those of our neighborhoods. or Jesus is not God, not alive, and this is all fake news. Then we are just one in billions with no purpose other than to live for today and get the most we can out of life!

In this "Sincerely Seen" moment for the dripping-wet Peter, I can just imagine that he was saturated with a driving will to make himself invisible to Jesus, as he had just tried to escape with an all-nighter of fishing. What might he have been trying to escape besides the craziness of Jerusalem? Maybe he was escaping from the plaguing and debilitating darkness haunting his thoughts as he remembered when he had denied that he had ever known Jesus. I think it would have been hard to see Jesus as he swam to shore, as Peter walked up to Jesus in silence, to another "charcoal fire." This same kind of fire, a "charcoal fire," had burned in the courtyard that night where Peter denied that he had ever "Sincerely Seen" Jesus, his friend!

No more running, Peter! You have been caught by THE "charcoal fire." And as Peter blinks away his blindness, he is left standing there in front of Jesus, who looks at him and tells him, "Get out of here, you little jerk! I am no friend of yours! Remember what you said? Remember that you cursed and swore and said, 'I do not know the man!'" (Matt. 26:74).

NO! Jesus did not say this! John, the author, would write that when they all got to shore, they saw that Jesus was cooking fish and bread and welcoming them, as Peter stood there silently dripping, and Jesus was saying, "Bring some of the fish you have just caught" (John 21:10).

Jesus welcomed them all! There was no pointing of fingers, no blaming, no shaming, no dismissing, and no canceling Peter's story! **Only LOVE!** There was no avoiding, no ignoring, and no pretending! **Only TRUTH! And Grace equals Love plus Truth.**

This was the only Grace that would be present at that "charcoal fire." And Peter knew it! It might have been too much for Peter, so he ran to help the other fishermen drag in the nets full of fish, which, incidentally, Jesus helped them catch. I wonder who counted the fish? Did Matthew count them? After all, Matthew was a tax collector. Or did Peter count them to get his mind off the sight of Jesus standing by a "charcoal fire" with a grill full of fish and bread? I can imagine Peter, rocked by the reality of Jesus dying on a cross, and then Jesus no longer being dead but alive. It only makes sense that Peter went to the counting of the fish and then chattered about the number of fish over and over again in awkwardness; maybe it was a ploy to avoid past events! I might be reading into this, but it still had to be an uncomfortable moment for Peter to see Jesus. I sure would have been trying to be on my best behavior! Was this John's way of honoring Peter? John had to know this was a shame-or-honor moment for Peter; it was the Middle Eastern way not to humiliate a brother in public. Was redemption found by Peter in the number of fish they caught because they listened to Jesus' voice and obeyed His call to throw the net on the other side of the boat? Or was redemption realized by Peter when he stood looking at Jesus with a greeting on His lips, asking Peter to join Him for breakfast—for the breaking of the bread?

Oh brother and sister, oh you who struggle to admit your issues to Jesus—by the way, I do too! Let us be rocked, refreshed, and renewed! Jesus knows our darkest places of denial and betrayal, of cursing and swearing, and Jesus stands at our very own "charcoal fire." I imagine Him saying, "Bring what you have, empty your nets, and come and have breakfast with Me." Amazing is the love of the Jesus Christ, who makes breakfast on the beach and then invites us to it!

For we are all, after all, including Peter, "Sincerely Seen."

Jesus Christ—the God Who Invites Us to Breakfast!

Scene (Seen) 48

The Breakfast of Loving Tightly and Holding Loosely

John 21:12–14

Jesus said to them, "Come and have breakfast." Now none of the disciples dared to ask him, "Who are you?" because they knew it was the Lord. Jesus came and took the bread and gave it to them, and did the same with the fish. This was now the third time that Jesus appeared to the disciples after he was raised from the dead. (*NRSV*)

There is nothing sweeter than having breakfast made for you over a charcoal fire on the beach with your friends! Think of it! Simon Peter, Thomas, Nathaniel, the sons of Zebedee, and two others were gathering on the beach. Think of the smell of fresh-grilled fish and bread wafting past their nostrils as they landed on the beach, collecting the 153 fish and bringing them ashore in the nets. The spray of the waters, the wind in their faces, the dawn of the sun with a new day, and of course, Jesus standing at the fire, having cooked their breakfast! What an offering of peace, given by the King of Kings and the Lord of Lords!

The only way in which forgiveness and reconciliation can truly occur is when a space is provided for them. I call it the **space of loving tightly and holding loosely**. People can be difficult; they operate out of either fear or pride. When given opportunity to make amends, many from different cultures will move back, avoid, or at

The Breakfast of Loving Tightly and Holding Loosely

least procrastinate in moving forward into the broken relationship. Jesus knew this. Granted, there are those few who move into conflict or awkward situations with a readiness to fight, but I would say that most stand frozen in fright or flee into avoidance at all costs!

Mary Magdalene, when she realized who Jesus was at the garden tomb, was one of the few to hurl herself into the arms of Jesus. She was begging him to tell her where Jesus was, thinking He was the gardener, and when He called out her name, she neither froze nor fled! Instead, she embraced Him as if she wanted Him never to leave her again, only to have Jesus say, "Don't keep clinging to Me, for I have not yet ascended to the Father; but go to My brothers and say to them, 'I am ascending to My Father and to your Father, to My God and your God'" (NRSV). Jesus had not yet finished His news; He wanted Mary to go tell the men that He was alive, and that He would be going to His Father and their Father, His God and their God.

In other words, Jesus considered them family, and He appointed Mary to give them the news. She had to learn that the first lesson of a life following Jesus is to love tightly and hold loosely. This is the lesson that we all must learn: we are not in control. So how then will you and I (and how will Mary) live our lives? Will we, will she, love fiercely and hold freely? Jesus challenges us, Mary, and those disciples with the very challenge that He was not exempt from learning. He had victory because He surrendered control—He was nailed to the cross and said these words: "Father, into Your hands I commit My Spirit." Jesus yielded, surrendered, and loved tightly and held "loosely" his life on this earth, all the way to the point of yielding his very Spirit into his Father God's hands. By "loosely" I mean Jesus didn't try to save his life, but he gave it up for all.

In John 10:4, Jesus says to His disciples, "When He puts forth all His own sheep, He goes ahead of them, and the sheep follow him because they know His voice." My point is that Jesus will never leave us alone to **love tightly and hold loosely**. Jesus the good Shepherd always leads His sheep, never leading them into a place that he hasn't been before them! I don't have to hold so tightly my situations or circumstances, the people I love or the people I struggle to love. I can know that God is in control—Jesus is in control. He is the good Shepherd. As Jesus yielded His own Spirit into God's hands, I, through Jesus, can learn to let go too.

Now, as Jesus fixes breakfast for his family and brothers, he sets the stage for Peter's own lesson about loving tightly and holding loosely. To love tightly is to love with all that one has (influence, service, emotion, strength, physical capability, spiritual intensity, and mental stamina). To hold loosely, for you or me, is to let go of control and realize we are not the ones in charge *all* the time. To hold loosely doesn't mean to ignore or avoid, but to love others with a no-strings-attached kind of love, with no guilt and no manipulation. Love means clearly setting another free to choose to love back—especially those who might have failed you. This is how Jesus loved. He loved freely, even though he is the God who is in control and Sovereign in all regards. Yet he chooses to love each of us freely, extravagantly, giving us the choice of a relationship with him.

This would be a day to be remembered by Peter and by all: breakfast on the beach, cooked by the Savior of the world, who knows how to love tightly and hold loosely with his nail-scarred hands. This seems impossible—this "love tightly and hold loosely kind of love. Christ has gone before us, even to the point of fixing breakfast on the beach for those who abandoned him. He loves tightly and holds loosely, giving us all the choice to say yes to his love. How has Jesus called you to breakfast with him? What is Jesus asking you to love tightly and hold loosely? It is the lesson of a lifetime, a lesson of love, and a lesson of service with enormous challenges. Jesus is fully aware of the sacrifice. That is why he tells his friends, "Come and have breakfast." They knew for sure that it was Jesus, their living Lord. They knew who he was:

Jesus Christ—King of Loving Tightly and Lord of Holding Loosely.

You might want to try breakfast with Jesus; it could possibly be the most freeing thing you do today!

Scene (Seen) 49

Uncovered and Loved

John 21:15–17

When they had finished breakfast, Jesus said to Simon Peter, "Simon son of John, do you love me more than these?" He said to him, "Yes, Lord; you know that I love you." Jesus said to him, "Feed my lambs." A second time he said to him, "Simon son of John, do you love me?" He said to him, "Yes, Lord; you know that I love you." Jesus said to him, "Tend my sheep." He said to him the third time, "Simon son of John, do you love me?" Peter felt hurt because he said to him the third time, "Do you love me?" And he said to him, "Lord, you know everything; you know that I love you." Jesus said to him, "Feed my sheep." (*NRSV*)

I love the ocean and rocking a baby; I love shady tree walks and coffee-drinking talks; I love water fountains and the majesty of mountains; I love my family and listening to them banter with one another or reading their "group" texts; I love watching snowflakes drift lazily down from the clouds; I love the hills of sunflowers in August and the autumn leaves that rustle in the fall breeze; I love watching kids eat spaghetti! I just love the random things of life! The list can go on and on; I'm sure you can think of 101 things that you love in this random life of ours.

But that's just the problem; in our English language, we have one word for all the people, animals, actions, and anything else in life that we love! Just one word: love! But not in the ancient Greek, and this brings us to our text. I have led many college students through the reading of this text, and always, at the end of reading, I ask the question, "Why is Peter 'hurt' after Jesus asked him the third time, 'Do you love me?'"

> **Before we endeavor to work through this text, take the time to think about that question, and maybe write down your thoughts.**

Inevitably, I always get the same answer in my classes when asking this question. "Peter was 'hurt' because Jesus kept asking him the same question, as if Jesus didn't believe him." I would partially agree: Jesus was asking Peter a question that hurt him, but let's look at the word "love" through the lens of the language.

"Simon, son of John, do you *agapao* me more than these?" The word *agapao* means "to welcome, to entertain, to be fond of, to love clearly" (Strong, 25). The word is connected with the love of God. Then Peter answers Jesus by saying, "Yes, Lord, You know that I *phileo* you" (Strong, 5368). *Phileo* means to approve, to like, to sanction; it is connected with brotherly love, (as Philadelphia is the City of Brotherly Love).

Jesus would then ask Peter the same question a second time: "Simon, son of John, do you *agapao* me more than these?" And Peter would respond again, "Yes, Lord, You know that I *phileo* you." In other words, Jesus asked Simon Peter two times whether he *agapao* Him, and both times Peter's response was, "Yes, you know that I *phileo* you." Both times there was a disconnect.

Jesus used *agapao,* and Peter used *phileo,* so there was some sort of disconnect. Dr. Bruner, for whom I have the greatest respect, would write that both words are synonymous in John's vocabulary. Both are words of love.

But if I took complete freedom to connect this text with our culture and wondered, in the extravagantly written manner of comedic relief, I think it would be like when a young man professes his love to his girl and she responds with, "Well, I like you." You know that relationship isn't connecting on the same level, to say the least, and that young man better quit while he's ahead! Have you ever been in that position? It's awkward!

Could it be that Jesus is asking Peter if he loves Him, and Peter is responding, "You know I am fond of you?" The point is that Jesus asked three times, and three times, at the only other mention of a "charcoal fire" in Scripture, Peter was challenged about his heart toward Jesus! Peter couldn't hide, and neither can you or I!

The charcoal fire was a reminder or disclosure of Peter's conscience about denying Jesus just a few days before, when he was standing in the courtyard where Jesus had been arrested. John's very own words in the boat, "It's the Master," had to be a reminder to Peter of his own denial of even a faithful brotherly love to Jesus, enough to make Peter subconsciously throw on the cover of his robes as he dove into the waters to swim to Jesus. And probably Peter's answer to Jesus' questions were like signal flares in his heart, disclosing to Peter his own hidden secrets. Peter knew that he had failed at even being a friend to Jesus when he betrayed Him at the courtyard fire on good Friday! He did not love Jesus the way Jesus loved him! In fact, Jesus would strip away all the covers of Peter's heart at this charcoal fire when he asked the question a third time, "Simon, son of John, do you *phileo* me?" Maybe the change of words by Jesus would have alerted Peter to the guilt-ridden feelings he carried. The conversation, short and sweet, is this:

> Jesus: Simon, son of John, do you love (*agapao*) Me?
> Peter: Yes, Lord, you know that I love (*phileo*) you.
> Jesus: Simon, son of John, do you love (*agapao*) Me?
> Peter: Yes, Lord you know that I love (*phileo*) you.
> Jesus: Simon, son of John, do you love (*phileo*) Me?

No wonder John would write that "Peter felt hurt because He had asked him the third time, 'Do you love [*phileo*] Me?'" Jesus' words would pierce Peter's heart because the third time, I believe, Peter knew he couldn't cover up, couldn't measure up, couldn't avoid, and couldn't fake his heart or past actions in front of Jesus as he stood there in front of that charcoal fire! Everyone standing around that fire knew Peter's denial, but lest any of us forget, all of them had fled the scene when Jesus was arrested in Gethsemane; all stood far away from the cross as Jesus was crucified (except for Mary and John); all hid in their homes hoping not to be associated with even the name of Jesus of Nazareth. Everyone standing there, including Peter, who had told Jesus, "Though all become deserters because of you, I will never desert you" (Matt. 26:33), had abandoned Jesus, denied Jesus, or not tried as hard as they could to *agapao* Jesus; they had failed Jesus. They failed to love Him clearly or dearly. I'm not judging, I do the same.

Peter's answer to Jesus was definitely an understatement. "Lord, you know all things; you know that I *phileo* you." Jesus knew all things about Peter and the rest of that motley sailing crew. He knew Peter would deny Him before it even happened. "Jesus said to him, 'Truly I tell you, this very night, before the cock crows, you will deny me three times. Peter said to him, 'Even though I must die with you, I will not deny you.' *And so said all the disciples*" (Matt. 26:34–35).

I had always thought that Peter was the only one who would say those things until the day I slowed down and read the words, "And so said all the disciples." I wonder if Matthew wanted to make sure the reader knew that *all* the disciples failed Jesus? Jesus knew Peter was covering up, maybe even trying to please Jesus, by running back to help with the nets and the fish; maybe Peter was even overcompensating to make up for the deep heart failures that were hidden in the core of his being—the haunting reality that he, Peter, couldn't love the way Jesus loved him? I wonder.

It wasn't only because Jesus asked Peter three times that he was hurt! It was because Peter came face-to-face with his Lord, who did not allow him to "save face" but instead made him come to the truth. Jesus knew all things, and yet through all of the questioning, never once did He quit believing in Peter. Each time that Jesus probed Peter's heart with His questions and pursued Peter long enough to help him come face-to-face with his broken failures, Jesus ALSO told him, "Tend my lambs," "Shepherd my sheep," and "Tend my sheep."

Uncovered and Loved

This strikes deep in my heart because so often I am ruled by performance. It is not about my works; it is not about my sacrifices! As God makes clear throughout the Scripture, "For You do not delight in sacrifice, otherwise I would give it; You do not take pleasure in burnt offering." (Is this a prophetic word about Peter's fish on the grill?) "The sacrifices of God are a broken spirit; a broken and contrite heart, O God, You will not despise" (Ps. 51:16–17).

Peter, in front of his six friends and Jesus, came to a place of reality. He could have fought it, could have given Jesus the silent treatment, could have ignored Jesus' questions and pretended not to hear them, could have argued with Jesus or just plain walked away, but he didn't! He freely admitted, "Lord, You know all things."

> **Will you and I come to Jesus with our cover-ups, our hidings, and our works (no matter how great or small they are) and look deep into His eyes, which can pierce a heart and soul with the same tenacity as the nails that pierced Jesus' wrists and ankles?**

"Lord, You know all things."

> **And then, after allowing Jesus to look into your heart and soul in front of your own charcoal fire of sorts, will you receive the love of Jesus and the charge of Jesus to go take care of His lambs and sheep?**

"Lord, You know all things."

I dare you and myself to stand before the charcoal fire and let the words Jesus spoke to Peter be spoken to us. Then, let us answer honestly.

We might find peace, and surely we will find *agapao*.

Jesus Christ—God of LOVE.

Scene (Seen) 50

The 2-C Dilemma

John 21:18–24

"Very truly, I tell you, when you were younger, you used to fasten your own belt and to go wherever you wished. But when you grow old, you will stretch out your hands, and someone else will fasten a belt around you and take you where you do not wish to go." [He said this to indicate the kind of death by which he would glorify God]. After this he said to him, "Follow me." Peter turned and saw the disciple whom Jesus loved following them; he was the one who had reclined next to Jesus at the supper and had said, "Lord, who is it that is going to betray you?" When Peter saw him, he said to Jesus, "Lord, what about him?" Jesus said to him, "If it is my will that he remain until I come, what is that to you? Follow me!" So the rumor spread in the community that this disciple would not die. Yet Jesus did not say to him that he would not die, but, "If it is my will that he remains until I come, what is that to you?" This is the disciple who is testifying to these things and has written them, and we know that his testimony is true. *(NRSV)*

"Jesus Loves Me," by Anna Bartlett Warner and William Batchelder Bradbury, is such a simple song: "Jesus loves me, this I know, for the Bible tells me so. Little ones to Him belong. They are weak, but He is strong. Yes, Jesus loves me, yes, Jesus loves me, yes, Jesus loves me, the Bible tells me so."

Jesus is strong in His love—for Peter, for John, and for all of us. Most certainly, in our last devotion we read about Peter's confession, "Lord, You know all things." In other words, I would imagine Peter has been challenged in his heart. Nothing is hidden with Jesus; nothing is covered up with Jesus. Jesus knew Peter denied Him; He knew Peter would do so even before that day. Jesus loves Peter when he is weak because Jesus is strong. Jesus knew all things.

The Psalmist writes: "O LORD, you have searched me and known me. You know when I sit down and when I rise up; you discern my thoughts from far away. You search out my path and my lying down, and are acquainted with all my ways. Even before a word is on my tongue, O LORD, you know it completely" (Pss. 139:1–4). There are no surprises with God. No, not one! Immediately after this heart-to-heart, with Jesus unveiling Peter's heart, Peter moves his gaze from Jesus to John, his buddy, "the one who had leaned back on His chest at the supper and said, 'Lord, who is the one who is betraying You?'" (John 21:20).

When Jesus and His disciples ate their food, the custom was that they would lie stretched out, resting on their left elbows and stretching their legs out diagonally—maybe on couches, or right on the floor. So the disciple next to Jesus, who could lean back on Jesus' chest, was John, who would have been to the right of Jesus, a favored position.

Now Peter is hearing for the first time how he will experience suffering. "You will stretch out your hands and someone else will fasten a belt around you and take you where you do not want to go." Peter turns around and, seeing John, asks Jesus, "What about this man?" This is what I love about Peter; I call him "No-Screens Peter!" He just says the thing that most people think but don't have the courage or bluntness to say. In other words, Peter was probably thinking, "Enough about me; what about John? Let's focus on him for a change." How many times have we each wanted to be away from the eyes of authority or our boss's scrutiny? How often do I send up the screen of defense when I hear what I don't want to hear or think about? And if not a screen of defense, then a screen of deflection or avoidance would be useful as well.

I have an example! I'm sitting in a seminary class, and I did not complete my Greek translation assignment. Our professor was calling on us, person by person and row by row, to translate one of the Greek sentences. Luckily, he had started on the other side of the classroom. We were each expected to read the numbered sentence of the text, in Greek, out loud, and then verbally translate it. I counted the sentences on the paper that we each had, and to my great relief, I saw there were eighteen sentences, and I was number nineteen in the class! I was off the hook, and thought, "Yes… thank You, God!" When the person in front of me finished the eighteenth sentence, to my dismay, Dr. Nelson said, "Next," and looked straight at me. While I had been busy calculating the number of sentences and the number of people in the class, I had not realized that there were sentences on the back of the page! I froze!

I know you might be thinking, "How did she ever get into seminary in the first place if she didn't think to turn the page?" I know…I'm sure Dr. Nelson was wondering the same thing as he sat there waiting for me to respond. I turned the page over, and there was my nineteenth sentence, staring me in my face. What was I to do? I could either try to fake it or be real. I knew, from countess mishaps (outside of Greek class) when I had tried to fake it in life, that I just didn't have a good "poker face" and wasn't good at a fake scene. And after all, I thought, "This is seminary; you can't fake it."

So I said, "Dr. Nelson, I do not have number nineteen completed. Actually, I did not do the assignment. I'm sorry." Everyone in the room froze—it was as if I was in an echo chamber.

Dr. Nelson said, "Excuse me, Mrs. Mason, what did you say?" (Note: I'm sure Jesus didn't say, "Excuse Me, Peter, what did you say?" as Peter stood there looking at John.)

Anyway, the room was silent, and I stated my plight again: "I'm sorry, Dr. Nelson, I did not complete the assignment."

"Very well, go on," he replied, and the student behind me had to complete number nineteen, which I'm sure he wasn't pleased with, because he too had been counting the sentences and preparing to do a great job with number twenty! It was a domino effect:

The 2-C Dilemma

no one in the entire row had completed their assignment, and they were all doing their calculations; I had blown everyone's cover! The moral of this story is that even our little messes have an impact on the many. And Peter's impact would make Him a real leader.

Back to our verses. Peter blurted out, "What about him?" And Jesus responded with a classic parental comment: "What's that to you? You follow me." In other words, if I were to reword this: "It doesn't matter about John or Matthew or the person down the street, Peter!" What matters to Jesus is He wants Peter to follow Him.

Peter had a comparison game going in his mind. Whenever I get into the comparison game with others, I remember this picture—this story. Jesus, Peter, and the other six disciples had just eaten, and I'm sure they were cleaning up. Jesus had just had a serious talk with Peter by the charcoal fire.

They get up, and Jesus, not quite finished with the task of Peter's training in leadership, tells Peter how his life will end. John overhears, and Peter knows that he is listening. How do I know John overhears? Well, he's writing it down later, so he must have heard it.

So—John overhears, Peter knows this, and just like in their competitive race to the tomb in chapter twenty, John is standing there following Jesus, and Peter compares and blurts out, "What about him?" We all have those kinds of "that's not fair" days.

Jesus' response is simple and to the point: "What's that to you? You follow me." I call it the "2-C Dilemma." We can either compare or celebrate. Take your pick, Peter, and stop looking at others (which, incidentally, is probably at the core of Peter's dark side—the temptation of people-pleasing)! Just follow Jesus.

Can you think of someone with whom you compare yourself these days? With whom do you line up?

Jesus asks us, "What's that to you? You follow Me."

What will it look like for you to follow Jesus no matter the cost, no matter the person in front of you or next to you or behind you?

Think about it. Are you comparing or celebrating? What's that to you? Follow Jesus.

What would following Jesus look like to you, regardless of others? Describe it.

Now, flip it around: instead of thinking about yourself, think about Jesus and why you would want to follow Him. Write about this. This is what really counts!

The interesting thing is that twice in these Scriptures, the word "remain" is written. I wonder how Peter thought about the word "remain" as he lived out his life, telling others about the Alive Jesus?

I wonder what it was like for John as he experienced the news of all of his friends being martyred for their faith, and he alone was left to write the story of "remain." I bet John would reflect on this word.

John would write, in John 15:9, "As the Father has loved me, so I have loved you; remain in my love."

This is the answer to the "2-C Dilemma." Truly, Jesus knew how to remain and would empower His friends to do the same. So—remain, my friends, remain.

"Therefore there is now no condemnation for those who are in Christ Jesus" (Rom. 8:1).

Jesus Christ—Lord Who Knows All Things!

Scene (Seen) 51

The Living God

John 21:23–24

So the rumor spread in the community that this disciple would not die. Yet Jesus did not say to him that he would not die, but, "If it is my will that he remains until I come, what is that to you?" This is the disciple who is testifying to these things and has written them, and we know that his testimony is true. *(NRSV)*

"So the rumor spread." It's amazing to think that even two thousand years ago there were rumors. Actually, John would write, "Therefore, this saying went out among the brethren." Some would write "rumor," but John wrote "saying," which is defined as "a word uttered by a living voice" (Strong, 3055). The word uttered back then was that Jesus was saying that John wouldn't die. But around 90 to 100 AD, John, wanting to clarify, wrote this account to make sure everyone knew the truth: the ONLY ONE LIVING BEYOND DEATH IS JESUS.

Why is this so important to John? It was important for many reasons. The first was that, at the time, he was writing this Gospel he had endured hearing about, in which Peter, the one whom John loved as a brother, dies upside down on a cross. They had been on many adventures together. He had watched Peter jump out of a boat to go to Jesus. He had watched Peter walk on water and then sink before Jesus grabbed him and saved him. He had seen Peter grapple with who he thought Jesus was when Jesus asked him that question, and Peter said, "You are the **Messiah**, the Son of the living God!" (Matt. 16:16). John must have reminisced many times about the name that Peter had given Jesus: "Son of the living God." Living God, or God of Life, is the name David declared as he was fighting Goliath in 1 Samuel 17:26: "For who is this uncircumcised Philistine that he should taunt the armies of the living God?"

I imagine John thinking back on the Scriptures and remembering this episode with David, and maybe even remembering enough to muster up his courage as he waited for the return of Jesus. John would remember the moments when Peter got called out by Jesus, when Peter told Jesus how things were going to go: "Peter took Jesus aside and began to rebuke Him, saying, 'God forbid it, Lord! This shall never happen to You'" (Matt. 16:22). Peter was telling Jesus "no way" as Jesus was speaking about being killed and rising on the third day. I wonder if John, overhearing this, looked back on the crucifixion and remembered standing at the foot of the cross with Jesus' mother, Mary, hearing Jesus telling him to take care of Mary and Mary to take care of John—they were to be family from then on. John saw Jesus yielding up His last breath, and I wonder what impact all these memories would have on old John later as he wrote this Gospel?

John would write these words to make sure everyone knew that he was an eyewitness. There were no questions in his mind. Jesus is the Living God. He IS alive. What impact did this have on John? Well, tradition has it that John might have been boiled in oil in Rome because of his faith and proclamation, and that he was miraculously healed. John was banished to Patmos to do mine work as a slave. He was then released and returned to Ephesus to live out his last years, teach, and write. Then John mentored Polycarp, a later church leader, and Ignatius of Antioch.

The point is, John never quit! **Why didn't he quit? He didn't quit because Jesus is the Living God! He writes, "This is the disciple who is testifying to these things and has written them, and we know that his testimony is true." John would never QUIT, because JESUS IS ALIVE.** It is one thing to believe in Jesus for this life, but it is quite another thing to believe Jesus is alive!

The Living God

I have had dear Christian friends who have lost hope and quit life. I remember the first time it happened. I got news of someone who was a strong follower of Jesus and had greatly influenced me as a young believer. She committed suicide, which I found out the night that she did it. I sat awake long after my husband and my infant son were asleep. I just couldn't sleep, plagued with the questions, "Why did she do this, since she believed in Jesus?" and "What is faith in Jesus about?"

In other words, this was my own crisis of faith, when I thought, "What is the use of believing?" It was one o'clock in the morning, and I still couldn't sleep, so I got out my Bible. As a young believer, I just cried out to God, asking Him to show me something, anything, to help me understand. Then I did what every one of us has done. I thumbed through all the pages, prayed, put my finger on a passage, and read.

Now, I want you to know, friends, that I am not ashamed of doing this! I was new at this Jesus faith, and all I knew was that this was His Word. So, flipping through the pages, I stopped, and without looking, I put my finger on a verse. It read, "If we have hoped in Christ in this life only, we are of all men most to be pitied" (1 Cor. 15:19). The Living God answered me. I read this over and over, along with the rest of the apostle Paul's words in 1 Corinthians 15, which teach the people of Corinth the utmost significance of the resurrection of Christ, and I realized that if my hope and belief in Christ were just to make me feel better in this life, then I should be pitied in my thinking, my believing, and my faith most of all!

John didn't quit, because he knew who he was. He remembered all of his friends and their adventures, with Jesus in the middle. And he KNEW without a shadow of doubt that Jesus was resurrected—alive—and He would return one day. "But now Christ has been raised from the dead, the first fruits of those who are asleep" (1 Cor. 15:20). Jesus is the FIRST FRUITS (we have had that devotion before), and Jesus is still the FIRST FRUIT, and He will always be the FIRST FRUIT.

Paul writes, "The last enemy that will be abolished is death" (1 Cor. 15:26). John knew Paul, and John knew Peter, and John knew Jesus, THE LIVING GOD. That's it. No reason to live just for this life, no reason to lose hope, no reason to do anything but wait for THE LIVING GOD, JESUS, and look forward each day to being able to get up and bring love, compassion, a listening heart, and faithful teaching to others in the confident expectancy of THE LIVING GOD.

How, then, shall you and I live out today? Where is your hope; where is my hope?

Jesus Christ—Messiah

Scene (Seen) 52

Oh, How Great!

John 21:25

> But there are also many other things that Jesus did; if every one of them were written down, I suppose that the world itself could not contain the books that would be written. (*NRSV*)

The stories of Jesus, if they were all written down, could not be contained in the world. Was this a saying back then? Like when we say, "Oh, it's raining cats and dogs" (which no one says anymore). This phrase doesn't mean it is actually raining animals; it means that it is raining very hard. What if John was trying to communicate to all who read his work the GREATNESS and the ENORMOUS HOLINESS of this living, breathing Jesus? John will write, "See how great a love the Father has given us, that we would be called children of God; and *in fact,* we are" (1 John 3:1). The words "how great" were actually an idiom, *potapos*, which meant "from what country or nation." Breaking down this sentence, we have: "See from-what-country-or-nation-or-world a love the Father has given us, that we would be called children of God." In other words, God's love for us is so **otherworldly** that it cannot be contained; it's out of the country or nation to understand this kind of love. I think this is what John, the beloved disciple, is trying to convey. "I suppose the world itself could not contain the books that would be written;" in other words, "There's just not enough space to write all there is to write about Jesus, the Living God."

> **How do we get this "out-of-world" perspective when it comes to faith in Jesus?**

Matthew would write to the Jewish people from his Jewish perspective in order to help them understand the greatness of Jesus, the Living God. He would be detailed in his prophecies, always pointing to the One—the Messiah—who was to come, then came and lived among them. Matthew was a shrewd businessman with an eye for the count, and he counted once and for all that Jesus was and is the Christ.

Mark was the "adolescent" of the group, not even an apostle. He would write with incredible urgency, as if to alert all who read his work of the One he walked next to with Peter. He wasn't into details, like Matthew. He seems to write in a hurry, with an "And-then-it-happened" kind of mentality, to try to show that Jesus was on the go, not standing still, and that Jesus the Son of God was the Living God. Mark might have been the one who came to warn Jesus at the Garden of Gethsemane that soldiers were coming. When Mark arrived, he found out that he was too late, and as all were fleeing, a soldier grabbed him. He fled without his robe, naked, to escape the impending tomb that was being brought down on Jesus the Nazarene.

"A young man was following Him, wearing nothing but a linen sheet over his naked body; and they seized him. But he pulled free of the linen sheet and escaped naked" (Mark 14:51–52). I wonder if, in Mark's eyes, Jesus was the Living-God-Hero of his time, and he wanted all to know it? Mark would spend a lot of time hanging out with Peter and the rest of the disciples as he learned to be a faithful follower of Jesus the Living God.

Luke was a methodical doctor, a learned man with a high degree of education, a traveler with Paul, and he interviewed many people who followed Jesus. Greek by birth, Luke would write detail after detail to help his Greek friends understand that this Jesus was no fake god, that this Jesus was the Living God. Writing about the details of the resurrection, the picture stories of Thomas, the women, and the healing of so many were Luke's strengths. He would write in the most educated Greek language, and he wanted all to know that Jesus was the Everlasting, True, and Fully Alive God!

Oh, How Great!

And then there's John, the beloved disciple. John had the uncanny ability to write with great detail, revealing how the signs of Jesus as God (the healings and the miracles) all pointed to Jesus and highlighted words of Jesus that taught who He really was: the I AM. John, like the eagle who can see a fish in a lake from a soaring distance above, swooping down with agility and grace and pluck that fish right out of the water, had the ability to see the GREAT big picture of Jesus as well as the mighty fine details of who Jesus was as the Living God. He was accurate in writing that there were not enough volumes in the world to tell who Jesus was, is, and ever shall be!

These last words by John, **"I suppose that the world itself could not contain the books that would be written,"** have a powerful solidity of truth and love; they are written clearly to tell all of the "Aliveness" of JESUS CHRIST! These words are etched in this last Gospel of truth, and they could not be written in a more truth-filled internet post, set to a more melodious song, or spoken more eloquently to the world in a court of justice! Think about all the wonder-filled moments you have ever had: a baby being born, being with a loved one when they die, a fresh breath of air after rain, a symphony of beauty heard under the great skies filled with stars, a child wondering at the beauty of a butterfly, the ocean sweeping onto the shoreline, a powerful desert storm, or the winds pummeling and bending the trees in a deep-thicketed forest.

I would state that all of these "wonder" moments pale in comparison with the powerful and beautiful Alive Jesus Christ walking with us, talking with us, and showing us His wonderful Shepherd way! And when you have had that moment of WONDER, I pray that you can get a glimpse of the TRUTH: that Jesus is Alive, that He is the Living God, and that His LOVE for you and me is so great that we are called "Children of God." May we never forget to be in wonder before our Living God, as His children! The Living God dances over His children—the Father, the Son, and the Holy Spirit. We too will dance one day.

Jesus, the Living God—the Wonder!
Oh, how great,
Oh, the exquisite hope,
Oh, the Peace that is Joy Standing Still,
Oh, the Joy that is Peace Dancing!

Write about something that you were in wonder about. Then think about Jesus, and expect to see Him around the next corner.

Jesus Christ—the God of Wonder! Epilogue

An epilogue is the last chapter of a book, but in this devotional, there is no final chapter!

Maybe you read one Scene a week, and with there being fifty-two scenes, it worked out perfectly that you completed the book in a year. If you chose to read it through at a different speed that is great as well. Either way these scenes have only just begun, for they carry on from generation to generation as the church continues. Consider these last two Scenes the epilogue of beginnings. Then, as you celebrate your new year, consider writing your own scenes of seeing the Lord Jesus in your life!

Epilogue
Scene (Seen) 53

As Eagles Fly!

Acts 1:3–11

After his suffering he presented himself alive to them by many convincing proofs, appearing to them during forty days and speaking about the kingdom of God. While staying with them, he ordered them not to leave Jerusalem, but to wait there for the promise of the Father. "This," he said, "is what you have heard from me; for John baptized with water, but you will be baptized with the Holy Spirit not many days from now." So when they had come together, they asked him, "Lord, is this the time when you will restore the kingdom to Israel?" He replied, "It is not for you to know the times or periods that the Father has set by his own authority. But you will receive power when the Holy Spirit has come upon you; and you will be my witnesses in Jerusalem, in all Judea and Samaria, and to the ends of the earth." When he had said this, as they were watching, he was lifted up, and a cloud took him out of their sight. While he was going and they were gazing up toward heaven, suddenly two men in white robes stood by them. They said, "Men of Galilee, why do you stand looking up toward heaven? This Jesus, who has been taken up from you into heaven, will come in the same way as you saw him go into heaven." (*NRSV*)

Do you ever think back to the last words a loved one said to you? These were probably the last words Jesus said to His friends before He ascended to heaven. His friends were most certainly perplexed as Jesus went up into the sky and out of their sight. And then, as if that were not enough to bewilder them, the angels standing next to them asked them why in the world they were still standing there looking up in heaven; Jesus had left. They were there to remind Jesus' friends to go and wait for the Holy Spirit to come upon them, and they did!

I had a friend once who was grieving the loss of one of his friends. I was staying with him and his wife, and one morning I sat out in front of their home to read and pray. They came out to be with me, and we sat quietly, drinking coffee. Finally, my friend asked me, "Kathy, what convinces you that Jesus is alive?"

I knew he was asking me because he was thinking about the friend he had just lost, and I think he was asking me because he was also thinking about his own faith. (He wasn't alone in those questions and thoughts.) I tried to be sensitive and ask him questions, but I could tell he just wanted to listen. I talked about a few times in my life when things that I knew couldn't have been coincidences had happened, which were moments orchestrated by the hand of the sovereign God—Jesus. I talked about the times when I sensed Jesus' Spirit and how He guided me in those life-and-death experiences, and then I asked him, "How do you know that Jesus is alive?"

He paused, and then the hurt and anger started to come out, along with the confusion (and I don't blame or fault him at all, because I have been there plenty of times myself). He said, "If Jesus is alive, then WHERE IS HE?" I knew he was referring to where Jesus was when his friend needed Him. I just sat quietly. Then he said again, with great passion, "Where is Jesus if He is alive? I mean, is He up on a planet, or is He hiding on some island? Where is He?"

I just sat there, because the three of us could not answer the question. Just then, something in the sky caught our eyes, and we saw three eagles flying in a triangular formation. Wondering if they were drones, we looked more intently, and my friend said, "What are those? They look like eagles…they aren't drones." And they definitely were birds—eagles. We kept looking at them, and my friend was googling to find out if anyone else was seeing them while his wife was looking up—eagles.

She said, "They are definitely eagles, but eagles don't fly together. That's weird." We all stared up in the sky, just watching them soar in a triangle formation, and then they were gone.

We all just looked at each other, incredulous, and I finally said to my friend, "Did we see three eagles for sure?"

He answered, "Yes, those were three eagles."

Then I asked, "Then where are they now?"

He started to answer when the reason I was asking this question hit him. "We saw the eagles, they were real, and now we don't see them," I said. "So did we really see eagles? We don't know where the eagles are, but they were real, and we saw them."

My friend, kind of getting agitated, said, "Kathy, I know your point."

And then, with tears in my eyes and love in my heart, I said, "I know the disciples saw the Risen Jesus. They were with Him off and on for forty days, and then, just like these eagles, they saw Him up in the sky, and He was gone. I believe His disciples—I believe that Jesus is real; I believe that He is good; I believe that He is in control because He is God; and I believe that He is love. I know they saw Him go, and then He was gone. This doesn't mean He doesn't exist. This just means I don't know where He is. This just means I don't have all the answers. This just means I am not in control. This just means I am not God. What I do know is that your friend knew Jesus, you know Jesus, and I know Jesus. What I do know is Jesus is alive, and Jesus loves me, you, and your friend."

This is the human story I think about when I read this story in Acts. This is not the end of the story by any means. In fact, for the disciples, this would be the beginning of their amazing adventures: full of healings and people believing their words, repenting, and returning to God through Jesus Christ. This would be the beginning of their hardships and the beginning of their great hopes. This was truly the beginning, and it all starts with Jesus and ends with Jesus!

It has been my great privilege to write this resurrection devotional because it has drawn me back to the beginnings of my faith, when I said yes to Jesus as a college student, as I continue to follow Him through life—a daughter of God, a wife, a mother and grandmother, a college professor, and a Young Life volunteer.

Jesus is alive, and this is the greatest news on the face of the earth!

I pray this will be a good reminder. There are plenty more stories to tell about our ALIVE Jesus and plenty more prayers to be uttered. Meanwhile, keep looking up, because one day He is going to return. Lately I have been reminding my college friends to figure out for themselves, **"What will it take for you to expect Jesus around the next corner?"** I am praying that any who read this will ask themselves the same question, and then go seek Him and tell others about our Living God and the hope we have of a resurrected life with our Jesus.

The Old Testament writer of 1 Kings records Solomon, who built the Temple in Jerusalem, as once saying, "But will God indeed dwell on the earth? Behold, heaven and the highest heaven cannot contain You, how much less this house which I have built!" He was wrong in thinking it was preposterous for God to dwell on the earth; Jesus Christ walked on earth—the One who called Himself the Son of God, the Son of Man.

But Solomon was right in saying, "Behold, heaven and the highest heaven cannot contain You." God is too big and too great to be held in a house built by men. God, in His infinite power, raised Jesus Christ from the dead. God ate fish with His friends, He passed out bread to His friends, He hugged children, He wept for His friends, and He walked through walls and closed doors to be with His friends. All wisdom, clarity of truth, gentleness, justice, mercy, forgiveness, holiness, and control belonged to Him as He walked with them. Jesus met them in gardens, He met them on mountaintops, He met them on the road to Emmaus, and He talked with them on the beaches. Jesus is Alive, and He promises that He is coming back. Solomon was right: "Behold, heaven and the highest heaven cannot contain You," and I say, **"And neither could the grave!"** *Amen and Amen!*

> What do you want to remember from this devotional? What is it about Jesus that most astounds you?
>
> How will you live differently because you expect Him around the next corner?
>
> Now go and tell a world that is filled with hopelessness and despair: JESUS IS ALIVE.

Jesus Christ—Victorious God!

Epilogue

Scene (Seen) 54

All Together in One Place— Happy Birthday!

Acts 2:1–13

When the day of Pentecost had come, they were all together in one place. And suddenly from heaven there came a sound like the rush of a violent wind, and it filled the entire house where they were sitting. Divided tongues, as of fire, appeared among them, and a tongue rested on each of them. All of them were filled with the Holy Spirit and began to speak in other languages, as the Spirit gave them ability. Now there were devout Jews from every nation under heaven living in Jerusalem. And at this sound the crowd gathered and was bewildered, because each one heard them speaking in the native language of each. Amazed and astonished, they asked, "Are not all these who are speaking Galileans? And how is it that we hear, each of us, in our own native language? Parthians, Medes, Elamites, and residents of Mesopotamia, Judea and Cappadocia, Pontus and Asia, Phrygia and Pamphylia, Egypt and the parts of Libya belonging to Cyrene, and visitors from Rome, both Jews and proselytes, Cretans and Arabs—in our own languages we hear them speaking about God's deeds of power." All were amazed and perplexed, saying to one another, "What does this mean?" But others sneered and said, "They are filled with new wine." (*NRSV*)

All Together in One Place—Happy Birthday!

I would be remiss not to include this epic adventure of new beginnings: Pentecost! I thought only Christians celebrated this day, fifty days after Easter. But Pentecost, or *Shavout,* as the Hebrews called it, was a great celebration for the Jewish people: the Feast of Weeks. It was a time for the Hebrews to celebrate the Torah. It was a great feast day of rejoicing about God's Word, as given to them at Mount Sinai.

> And from the day after the sabbath, from the day on which you bring the sheaf of the elevation offering, you shall count off seven weeks; they shall be complete. You shall count until the day after the seventh sabbath, fifty days; then you shall present an offering of new grain to the Lord. You shall bring from your settlements, two loaves of bread as an elevation offering, each made of two-tenths of an ephah; they shall be of choice flour, baked with leaven, as first fruits to the Lord (Lev. 23:15–17).

On that day, Pentecost, the Jewish people ate bread and celebrated their harvests with great joy. How does this have anything to do with their Torah? Well, for the Hebrew, I can imagine that there is nothing better than to "eat" or learn from God's Word. And, of course, a warm piece of bread made from the harvested wheat would be just how to celebrate! The Torah is still memorized by the devout Hebrew. They were to remember coming out of the wilderness and entering the promised land of Israel, they were to remember God's promises fulfilled, and they were to remember the anniversary of God giving Moses the Law on Mount Sinai. What a celebration—and a harvest is a fulfillment of promise!

Fifty days later, the disciples and others were in a very large room. It had to be large, considering that there were Jews from all of these lands: "Parthians, Medes, Elamites, and residents of Mesopotamia, Judea and Cappadocia, Pontus and Asia, Phrygia and Pamphylia, Egypt, and the parts of Libya belonging to Cyrene, and visitors from Rome." If one were to study these lands, one would soon come to understand that, quite possibly, all the nations of the earth were represented. This is astounding! There were Middle Easterners, Africans, Asians, Russians, Islanders, Greeks, and Europeans, who would eventually make their way to the Americas and the rest of the world. This is incredible to think through, for sitting in that room were representatives of the whole earth.

The simple statement written by Dr. Luke in the book of Acts is profound: "They were all together in one place." How amazing and glorious are these seven words! God the Father had planned for this day, and Jesus had prayed for this day, "As you, Father, are in me and I am in you, may they also be in us, so that the world may believe that you have sent me" (John 17:21). Now the Spirit would fulfill this day! What an incredible moment for all to be in that room, hearing the same winds whisking through the room, with flames of fires anointing their minds and their hearts to new beginnings!

Luke would continue to write that God's Spirit gave them the ability to understand one another. Now that's a feat! All of them in one room, hearing different languages, understanding one another—it would be like having a dream of heaven on earth. But this was no dream—this was reality! Some would try to discount it by saying that those in the room had been drinking—the world will never understand the work of the Spirit—but Peter and those people knew different. God's Spirit was taking center stage for the purpose of drawing all men and women to Jesus Christ and bringing heaven to earth. After all, the Hebrew people knew that God had been named by the Old Testament leader, Ezra. Ezra was the one who would lead the Hebrews back to Jerusalem from Babylon to build the temple that Jesus Christ would walk through with His friends. The name of God that Ezra called out to was **Elohim Shamayim Yara—the God of heaven and earth** (Ezra 5:11)!

Now this reality was no longer for just a few women and men. This was indeed a new beginning as over three thousand people surrendered their hearts to Jesus, their Lord, that day. It was no longer to be a secret. The followers were being thrust onto the

All Together in One Place—Happy Birthday!

center stage of world history to testify that Jesus died but they had seen Him come back to life, and now the Holy Spirit was sealing hearts that day and forever. Oh, what a day that must have been. Oh, what a day we must always remember, for it is our great hope—to be all together in one place in the midst of the **God of heaven and earth!**

Those people were "Sincerely Seen" by the Lord that day; the Spirit of God rested over each of their heads. It isn't a coincidence that there were flames of fire hovering over their heads, for on that day, over a thousand years before, God had rested on Mount Sinai in fire and smoke, as it is written, "Now Mount Sinai was wrapped in smoke, because the LORD had descended upon it in fire; the smoke went up like the smoke of a kiln, while the whole mountain shook violently" (Exod. 19:18).

Moses would receive the Law, the Torah, that day, in the middle of a fiery mountain, which is the reason for Pentecost. Is this a coincidence? No! This was the Father God's plan to help His children see that Jesus was more than a poor carpenter from Nazareth. God's plan was to help all the nations of the earth to believe that Jesus was, is, and ever more will be the **God of heaven and earth.** This was the plan of God the Father—to remind His children that He would never leave them alone. His Holy Spirit would relentlessly break through all darkness, all closed rooms, all nations, and all tongues until "all together in one place," Jesus Christ would be praised.

God's Spirit is, as Dr. Dale Bruner writes, "the shy Member of the Trinity." The Holy Spirit is the One who points to the Father and the Son. "The work of the Holy Spirit is the honoring of Jesus Christ...The Holy Spirit does not center on the Holy Spirit" (Bruner, 2001, 11,15).

This shy Holy Spirit brought clarity to the heart and soul of each person there—like the winds in that ancient room, sweeping through it like a broom and cleaning it—and entered the heart of everyone present. The goodness of that moment was the greatest advent of the most incredible birthday party on the face of the earth!

I've had many a birthday party to celebrate many dear, beloved friends and family. Think back with me to your favorite birthday party, and then multiply the magnitude of your experience by the number of stars in the heavens. Then you and I might understand the magnitude of that great Pentecost day! It was as if the Holy Spirit wanted to shout out, "Come all ye together and bow down on this day—the day of the LORD. Come and sing, for He is your King. He is **Elohim Shamayim Yara—the God of Heaven and Earth!**"

The One who is shy but bold, the Holy Spirit, proclaims on the day of Pentecost, "Come and hear," which Peter proclaims to thousands of pilgrims who have come to celebrate the Feast of Weeks. I will always wonder if—on that day, as the room was filled with the presence of the Living God's Spirit and the breath of God entered into the hearts and souls of each one there—Peter remembered Jesus' words, "Feed My lambs…Tend My sheep…Feed My sheep" (John 21:16–17). Jesus had said those words to Peter on the beach that day, and now it was time. It was time for Peter to rise up, go out, and feed the lambs and sheep. I imagine that this was Peter's "no more self-centering, all-about-me" moment, as he would proclaim Jesus the Lord God, and thousands would repent and rejoice. What a day, oh, what a day, that "happy birthday, church" day!

May we take heed and intentionally be "all together" as we go forward to proclaim Jesus our living **God of Heaven and Earth.** He is the One who sincerely sees into the hearts of every man, woman, and child. He is the One who was sincerely seen by His beloved disciples, both men and women. And He is the One who sincerely sees us for who we are—we who long to see and be seen, **Sincerely Seen,** by the Creator of heaven and earth. Will you join the great assembly? Jesus is coming back, and His Spirit will no longer have to be shy, for it is written that on that day:

All Together in One Place—Happy Birthday!

"Therefore, God exalted him even more highly
And gave him the name
That is above every other name,
So that at the name given to Jesus
Every knee should bend,
In heaven and on earth and under the earth,
And every tongue should confess
That Jesus Christ is Lord,
To the glory of God the Father" (Phil. 2:9–11).

Happy Birthday, Church! Amen and Amen!

To God the Father, Jesus Christ the Son, and the Holy Spirit be all glory, forever and ever!

Jesus Christ—Elohim Shamayim Yara—the God of Heaven and Earth

The Finish of Scenes (Seens)

It's only fitting that in studying these four Gospels, I have discovered some of the evidence of Christ being alive. Matthew, a tax collector and accountant, or Luke, a research doctor, might have been the ones who would be interested in the evidence of hope. But the books of Mark and John are not to be discounted. They, too, are the records of the young and the old, writing eyewitness accounts of Jesus Christ—"my God and my Lord." Below, I have recorded this evidence, taken from the study of the resurrection of Christ in much of the Scripture.

Evidence of Jesus Sincerely Seen

1. Detectives use details to get to the bottom of truth. Any time details are given in a story, they are scrupulously recorded, down to the time and the he said/she said details. The Gospel writers would write details that were pertinent to their own personalities. Details are evidence. An example would be "153 fish" in John 21. This is evidence in that John deemed it important to count what would have been important to fishermen. Evidence usually entails detail that matches with the person reporting it. Evidence also matches up details.

Here is how I picture details that don't seem to quite line up in the Gospels: Picture two hands held up, facing each other at the fingertips, a few inches apart. There is space between the fingers. That space represents the differences in the details recorded by each Gospel writer and the spaces left open for the personality of each Gospel writer. The spaces are also there for the reader to exercise faith! We will never have proof. *We will have evidence of the risen Christ. We must exercise faith.*

That the details don't line up completely, I think, is evidence that the Gospel writers were telling the truth. They didn't care if they completely lined up, because they were telling the truth. To those reading these stories later, details would seem to be a problem if they didn't completely line up. AND if you were the one trying to prove they were accurate, you would make sure they lined up perfectly. But these authors did not try to force anything! The writings are not forced into a perfect fit. Instead, they are stories with details that pertain to the person writing the Gospel. Details show the reality of truth written by four different personalities. They leave space for their human-related truths, and they leave space for faith.

2. The fact that it was reported that the guards lost their prisoner was ridiculous. These were no ordinary guards. They were centurion guards who were notoriously good at their jobs. If they lost their prisoners, they would lose their lives. The tomb had not been robbed, and the guards were not asleep. The tomb was empty, and the guards had to report it.

3. The guards, in fact, had sealed the tomb because Jesus was reported dead, not semiconscious and then revived later. This is evidence that Jesus was truly dead, and therefore was resurrected from the dead.

4. If Matthew wanted to "beef up" his story, he would not have written that women were the primary witnesses. There had to be at least two witnesses, and women were not trusted as witnesses. In Greek, Roman, and Hebrew culture, women had no voice. YET Matthew wrote the truth. One would leave out this info if they were trying to substantiate the resurrection of Christ.

5. If the disciples wanted to "fake" the resurrection of Jesus, they would not have doubted themselves or shown any doubt. But in fact, numerous times in the Gospels, it was reported that the disciples doubted that Jesus was alive. If I were trying to convince someone of something, I certainly wouldn't have shown a shadow of doubt. The Gospels are honest in their reports of the disciples doubting—even after they saw Jesus!

The Finish of Scenes (Seens)

6. Over five hundred people were reported to have seen Jesus alive. If this had been some kind of PTSD on the part of the disciples, certainly not all five hundred people would have had the same emotional trauma. Many of these people died because they refused to state that they had NOT seen Jesus after He had been crucified.

7. The very fact that each Gospel is different is evidence of the reality of the resurrection, since four men had reported it as true from their various points of view.

8. So where are the manuscripts stating the fact that Jesus was NOT resurrected?

9. The world changed much of its calendar and ways of life because of Jesus' death, burial, and resurrection from the dead.

10. Many times, I have experienced "coincidences" that cannot be accounted for except by the fact that GOD is alive.

11. The disciples and thousands of believers have died martyr deaths because of their belief in the risen Christ.

12. The prophecies of Jesus in the Old Testament, over seventy of them, have been clearly personified in Jesus Christ.

13. I have watched others come to faith in Jesus Christ—the risen Lord. Their testimonies are credible.

14. My life has been changed permanently. I had no hope, and now I have hope.

15. As the Apostle Paul would write to the Corinthians, "If for this life only we have hoped in Christ, we are of all people most to be pitied" (1 Cor. 15:19). The hope of life eternal has not been destroyed by all of the persecutions, deaths of loved ones, and brokenness of the world. I have friends and family who have experienced death, seen Jesus as they were dying, and told me, "Kathy, don't worry about me. I will be okay. I'll see you soon."

My friends, this is by no means an exhaustive account of the evidence of the Alive Jesus. These are just a few examples. Use this time to think of your own, and then share them with me and others. The question is—what happens afterward? You—we—are left with a response to the God who gave us His All. Will we surrender and lay down our lives to serve Jesus at any cost—as these wonderful heroes of the faith did?

And then we will be able to—*Selah*!

Jesus Christ—Sincerely Seen

Note from the Author

Dear Fellow Sincerely Seen Friends,

I want to take this moment to thank you for the great adventure of walking through the Scriptures of the glorious resurrection of our Lord Jesus. As many times as I have read through these incredible stories, conversations, and thought-provoking words, I am always comforted by them. My heart and my mind remember of the truth, which is that "I am His beloved, and He is my beloved" (Song of Sol. 6:3). I pray that these will be the words you will hear over and over again. You and I are sincerely seen by the God. He is Elohim YHWH. You and I are sincerely seen and loved by the God. The Hebrew word that is my favorite is: El Ra'ah, which means God our Shepherd. You and I are sincerely seen in our worst days and our best days, in the trials before us, in pestilence, wars, and rumors of wars. You and I are sincerely seen for the purpose of having our eyes, our hearts, our minds, and our souls opened to sincerely see the God of Heaven and Earth.

I want to thank all who have helped me in this process: my husband, sons, daughters-in-law, and grandchildren, who have encouraged me to write down my words, my "cry out to God" moments, and my hilariously joyful moments when I realized that I was sincerely seen by the God of the universe.

I want to thank my mentor and her husband, Mary and Bob Malouf, who have been instrumental in my life of faith and ministry.

I want to thank my "small group" gals, who have always encouraged me, as well as all of the young friends I lead and mentor in Young Life.

I want to thank my sweet, dear friends: Patti, Rick, Orbi, Nikki,

Bailee, Tomasa, Mare, Dan, Carol, Travis, Brenda, Paul, Maree, David, and Dr. Clavell and Susan Barnfield at Arizona Christian University, who believed in my writing beyond my understanding. All of them have pressed me to write when I didn't think I had anything to say. God has used them all in my life to remind me to walk steady with Jesus.

I want to thank Dr. Frederick Dale Bruner and his brilliant wife, Kathy, who I am confident has put her hands to her forehead and groaned out loud as she read over this work of mine. They have been an incredible gift to me—I imagined them to be modern-day C.S. Lewis and Joy for me as they labored in truth and love over my work. I cannot thank them enough!

I leave you with these words: Christ is our Everything—our Alive God. He will sincerely return, and when He does, He will gather us together, and we will sincerely see Him—all together—seeing GOD! There will be no more loving tightly and holding loosely, because we will all sincerely have it all: the glorious splendor of being before the Father, the Son, and the Holy Spirit. We will no longer be cracked vessels with wax filling the seams. We will be vessels of honor filled with the glory of God, who heals all brokenness and all fractured vessels. We will truly be completed vessels—His image bearers made whole—fully loved and fully seen because we will **sincerely see God**.

Until that day, may the peace of Christ that is joy standing still and the joy of Christ that is peace dancing be before you, after you, with you, and in you all your days.

Kathy Mason

(**Put your name here**) _____ is Sincerely Seen.

Bibliography

Barclay, William, *The Gospel of John, Vol.2.* The Westminster Press, 1975.

Barclay, William, *The Gospel of Luke.* The Westminster Press, 1975.

Bruner, Frederick Dale, *The Gospel of John, A Commentary.* Grand Rapids: William B. Eerdmans Publishing Company, 2012.

Bruner, Frederick Dale, *Matthew Commentary, Volume 2 The Church Book. Grand Rapids:* William B. Eerdsman Publishing Company, 2014.

Bruner, Frederick Dale and Hordern, William, *The Holy Spirit Shy Member of the Trinity.* Wipf and Stock Publishers, 2001.

Edwards, Gene. *Silas.* Tyndale House Publishers.

Schulweis, Rabbi Harold, *The Hidden Matzah* - https://www.myjewishlearning.com/article/the-hidden-matzah/

Spurgeon, Charles. "Exposition of Psalm 32." Blue Letter Bible.

Spurgeon, Charles, *A Sermon (No.1835) Delivered on Lord's Day Morning,* Metropolitan Tabernacle, Newington, April 12, 1885. (Hebrews 7:4).

Stoner, Peter, *Science Speaks*, Josh McDowell Ministries, *Did Jesus Fulfill Old Testament Prophecy*, March 28,2018, https://www.josh.org/jesus-fulfill-prophecy/

Strong, James. Strong's Exhaustive Concordance of the Bible, Greek Dictionary of the New Testament. Abingdon Press, 1890.

About the Author

Kathy Mason and her husband, Richard, have lived, loved, and served youth in their community of Phoenix, Arizona, with a continued vision of hopeful expectation for over forty years. They are well aware of God's great love for them as they have four sons and lots of family to share that love. Kathy has a Masters of Arts in Theology from Fuller Theological Seminary and continues to serve in Young Life as volunteer staff and trainer. She teaches at Arizona Christian University as an Assistant Professor of Biblical Studies and Theology and has written several biblical and ministerial classes, including one of the Bible minor classes; *God's Image Bearers, Humanity's Story*. She serves as the ACU Young Life College Director and her great joy is wrapped up in serving and training college students in the truth of the gospel, service projects, laughter, adventures, and practical methods to become servant leaders in their communities.

Made in the USA
Monee, IL
04 February 2023